Slow
Cooker

Slow Cooker

100 tried and true recipes

First published in 2012

LOVE FOOD is an imprint of Parragon Books Ltd

Parragon Inc.
440 Park Avenue South, 13th Floor
New York, NY 10016

www.parragon.com/lovefood

ISBN: 978-1-4723-2208-1

Printed in China

New photography by Mike Cooper
New recipes by Robin Donovan
Introductions by Sarah Bush

Notes for the Reader
This book uses standard kitchen measuring spoons and cups. All spoon and cup measurements are level
unless otherwise indicated. Unless otherwise stated, milk is assumed to be whole, butter is assumed to
be salted, eggs are large, individual vegetables are medium, and pepper is freshly ground black pepper.
Unless otherwise stated, all root vegetables should be washed and peeled before using.

For the best results, use a meat thermometer when cooking meat and poultry—check the latest
USDA government guidelines for current advice.

Garnishes and serving suggestions are all optional and not necessarily included in the recipe
ingredients or method. The times given are only an approximate guide. Preparation times differ
according to the techniques used by different people and the cooking times may also vary from
those given. Optional ingredients, variations, or serving suggestions have not been included in
the calculations.

Recipes using raw or very lightly cooked eggs should be avoided by infants, the elderly, pregnant
women, and people with weakened immune systems. Pregnant and breast-feeding women are
advised to avoid eating peanuts and peanut products. People with nut allergies should be aware
that some of the prepared ingredients used in the recipes in this book may contain nuts. Always
check the packaging before use.

Vegetarians should be aware that some of the prepared ingredients used in the recipes in this book
may contain animal products. Always check the package before use.

CONTENTS

Introduction

It's abundantly clear why slow cooking has been a revered cooking technique since ancient times. It is, simply, the best way to produce vegetable dishes with deep flavor and meat so tender it falls from the bone. But with our busy modern lives, who has the time to tend to a pot simmering on the stove all day? Slow cookers are a welcome convenience for anyone who must be out of the house all day, but who wants to return to a delicious, ready-to-eat, home-cooked meal in the evening.

Since its invention in the 1970s, the slow cooker, or crockpot, has gained a reputation as a great set-it-and-forget-it countertop electric "casserole" for producing finished meals with minimal effort. But the slow cooker isn't just another one-trick appliance providing convenience at the expense of flavor. In fact, it has the ability to produce dishes—from appetizers to desserts—that taste fantastic. As meat, stock, vegetables, and herbs simmer together, their flavors emerge, intensify, and marry into an enticing whole.

The slow cooker is, of course, ideal for making flavor-packed stocks and soups, turning economical cuts of meat into rich stews, and transforming dried beans and hardy vegetables into wholesome meals. However, it is also great for cooking more delicate meats, fish, and vegetables, because the ingredients are cooked gently, without being broken down. More surprising is that the slow cooker is a great way to cook cakes and other desserts. It comes in handy when you don't want to heat up your kitchen during hot weather or if you are using your oven for something else—such as a turkey or a roast for a festive dinner.

Moreover, because the slow cooker uses very little electricity (less than a lightbulb!), it is both safe and economical to turn it on in the morning and leave it unattended all day. And because the temperature is low and constant, most dishes won't overcook, even after being left for 8 hours or more. What could be better than to arrive home after a long day to a meal that's ready to eat?

Choosing the right slow cooker for your family

The vast array of slow cookers available is enough to make your head spin. From tiny 1-quart models to giant 6-quart pots capable of feeding a small army, each available with or without a myriad options and special features, it can take a little research to determine which slow cooker is right for your family.

Quality in any price range

Slow cookers vary widely in price, from the most basic and inexpensive models to high-tech computerized machines that will put a serious dent in your wallet. The good news is that it is possible to find a good-quality slow cooker in any price range. Small models with only the most basic settings are surprisingly affordable. The larger you go and the more bells and whistles you add, the more you can expect to pay.

Size matters

One of the most important considerations in choosing a slow cooker is volume. To determine the size that is right for you, think about how many servings you'll need to make at one time. A 4-quart slow cooker is ideal for a family of four or five, while a smaller 2-quart cooker might be perfect for a couple. Larger cookers are great for large families, people who entertain frequently or advance planners who like to cook a big pot of something and freeze leftovers for future meals.

Oval or round?

While for most dishes—soups, stews, and the like—the shape of the slow cooker is irrelevant, some dishes are better suited to a particular shape of slow cooker. Oval slow cookers can easily fit big roasts, turkey breasts, leg shanks, and other large cuts of meat. On the other hand, if you plan to make a lot of cakes in your slow cooker, a round one is probably a better bet. Give some thought to the types of dish you will most probably cook in your slow cooker and choose a model accordingly.

Programmability

The most basic slow cooker models offer only three settings: high, low, and off. These models are inexpensive and work just fine. The downside is that they require you to set a separate timer and, more significantly, to be around to turn them off when the cooking time is up.

More expensive models often offer programming features that range from multiple time/temperature settings (such as "high 4 hours" or "low 8 hours") to an automatic switch-to-warm feature.

Others allow for you to set your own parameters for temperature and timing down to the minute. The more control you have over the settings, the more flexibility you'll get from your cooker— and the more you'll pay for the privilege.

If you plan to use your slow cooker mostly when you will be around the house, a basic model may suit you well. If, on the other hand, you hope to set your cooker in the morning before heading off to work for the day, consider one that includes a built-in timer and that will automatically switch to warm when the time is up.

Versatility

Most slow cookers come with a ceramic cooking vessel that is too porous for use on the stove. There are, however, a few high-end models with cooking inserts that can go from stove to slow cooker and back again. You'll pay a pretty penny for this luxury, but you'll save time and energy by not having to transfer ingredients from one pot to another and, even better, you'll reduce the number of dishes you need to wash.

Portability

Some slow cookers are portable and come fitted with hinged locking lids, carrying handles, and specially designed carrying cases and straps to help you transport food safely and easily.

Cleaning, maintenance, and safety

Be sure to read the instruction manual that comes with your slow cooker and always follow the manufacturer's guidelines for cleaning and maintaining your slow cooker.

While the glass lid of many slow cooker models is dishwasher safe, the ceramic cooking vessel that comes with most models is not. This is because the ceramic material that is used to make the vessel is porous, which is what makes it retain heat. Submerging it in water for long periods will cause it to absorb water, which will have a negative effect on its ability to retain heat. Unless your slow cooker's manual specifically says that it is dishwasher safe, wash it by hand and never leave it submerged in water for any length of time. If you encounter stuck-on food, fill the vessel with warm soapy water and let it soak for a few hours, then scrub out the stuck-on food.

Be careful never to plunge the hot ceramic pot into cold water, because this sudden temperature change may cause it to crack. Instead, fill it will warm water or, better still, let the pot cool before attempting to clean it.

The electric base, of course, should never be submerged in water. To clean it, unplug it and then use a damp sponge or cloth to wipe off any food that may have dripped onto the outside of the cooker.

The outer casing and lid may become very hot during cooking, so do be sure to place the cooker so that it is not too close to or touching any walls, curtains, cords, or other potentially flammable items when it is in use. Use oven mitts when touching any part of the slow cooker after it has been on for any period of time.

Always keep refrigerated foods cold until you are ready to add them to the slow cooker. If using frozen meat, poultry, fish, or shellfish, it is best to thaw it thoroughly before adding to the slow cooker. If you choose to add it while it is still frozen, you may need to adjust the final cooking time to be sure that the meat is thoroughly cooked.

What to cook in your slow cooker

Slow cooking certain cuts of meat over a long period of time makes them falling-off-the-bone tender, but you have to be sure to choose the right cuts. Very lean cuts, such as loin or sirloin, will dry out and become stringy in the slow cooker. Fattier cuts, such as chuck, shoulder, shank, and rump are better suited to low-and-slow cooking. Likewise, the dark meat portions of poultry (drumsticks, thighs, and wings) are better suited to the slow cooker, although breasts can be delicious if they are first browned in a skillet, well-seasoned, and cooked on low.

Of course, beans (see Food Safety Note) are also perfect for long, slow cooking. Hearty bean stews and vegetarian chili dishes, like those made with meat, become thick, rich, and deeply flavored after several hours in the slow cooker.

But it's not just high-protein foods, such as meat and beans, that are great cooked in the slow cooker. Vegetables, too, turn deeply flavored and tender after long slow braising. Choose hardy vegetables, such as potatoes, onions, carrots, turnips, winter squashes, and fennel. These won't disintegrate with the long slow cooking, but will be fork-tender and rich with the other flavors, herbs, and spices included in your recipe.

Food Safety Note

Dried beans cooked in the slow cooker have been linked to food poisoning. To be safe, soak dried beans for at least 5 hours prior to cooking, and then drain and rinse them, place them in a saucepan, cover with cold water, bring to a boil over medium-high heat, and cook at a rapid boil for at least 10 minutes. Remove from the heat, rinse, and drain one more time, and then place the beans in the slow cooker, cover with at least 1 inch of cold water and cook on low, covered, for about 8–10 hours, until tender. To prevent the beans from becoming tough, do not add salt until after cooking.

Tips for success with your slow cooker

Don't make the mistake of thinking of your slow cooker as a "dump-and-go" meal solution. Yes, the slow cooker allows for you to "set it and forget it," but many foods will benefit greatly from being prepared before going into the slow cooker. For instance, browning meat gives it a caramelized crust that contributes to the overall flavor of the dish and seals in the meat's juices, keeping it from drying out during cooking.

Browning meat before adding it to the slow cooker also renders a good deal of the fat, so it is recommended especially for dishes containing fresh ground meat, which might otherwise be too greasy.

Likewise, sautéing onions and garlic before adding them to the slow cooker deepens their flavor and, therefore, the taste of the finished dish. Adding spices to the sautéed onions and garlic and letting them cook for a moment or two will also help the flavors of the finished dish to marry.

Sometimes you can't wait all day for a dish to cook, and in these instances, cooking on high for a short period of time is appealing. If, however, you've got time to spare and a recipe gives alternative times for cooking on low or high settings, your best bet is usually to choose the longer, slower cooking. The longer and slower your food cooks, the more time it has to develop the depth of flavor that makes it especially delicious.

Keep in mind that, because slow cooker lids are designed to be more or less airtight, sauces and stocks won't reduce the way they do on the stove. For this reason, while it may seem counter-intuitive, adding too much liquid to a dish can render meat dry, vegetables flavorless, and sauces bland. Because the slow cooker retains all of the ingredients' natural moisture, a minimal amount of added liquid is sufficient for most dishes.

If, however, you are cooking a dish where you'd like the end result to include a thick sauce, try setting the lid of the slow cooker ajar for the last hour or so of cooking, thus allowing for steam to escape and the liquid to reduce. Don't do this too early, however, or you'll lose too much of the heat and your food won't cook through properly.

Cook it slow

All of the recipes in this book are designed to be easy to use—with short ingredient lists and minimal steps—but they never skimp on flavor. Whether your goal is to simplify weekday dinner preparations for your family or to impress guests with a meal that seems to have taken a lot more effort to prepare than it did, you'll find the inspiration and recipes you need right here. Happy slow cooking!

CHAPTER 1
SOUPS & APPETIZERS

Chicken Noodle Soup 15

Chicken Tortilla Soup 16

New England Clam Chowder 19

Shrimp Bisque 20

Salmon Chowder 23

Vietnamese Beef Noodle Soup 24

Tomato & Lentil Soup 27

Italian Bread Soup with Greens 28

Greek Bean & Vegetable Soup 31

Tuscan White Bean Spread with Roasted Garlic 32

Warm Chickpea Salad 35

Pears Stuffed with Blue Cheese 36

Stuffed Cabbage Rolls 39

Stuffed Chile Peppers 40

Sweet & Sour Chicken Wings 42

Spicy Chicken & Cheese Dip 44

Chicken Quesadillas 47

Mango Beef in Lettuce Cups 48

Beef & Chipotle Burritos 51

Beef Empanadas 52

CHICKEN NOODLE SOUP

serves **4**

1 onion, diced
2 celery stalks, diced
2 carrots, diced
2¼ pounds oven-ready chicken
3 cups hot chicken stock
4 ounces dried egg tagliatelle
salt and pepper, to taste
2 tablespoons chopped fresh dill,
 plus extra to garnish

Tales that this soup can cure a cold may be far-fetched, but a classic chicken soup is one of the most soul-warming recipes you can make.

1. Put the onion, celery, and carrots into the slow cooker. Season the chicken all over with salt and pepper and place on top. Pour the stock over the chicken, cover, and cook on low for 5 hours.

2. Leaving the juices in the slow cooker, carefully lift out the chicken and remove the meat from the carcass, discarding the bones and skin. Cut the meat into bite-size pieces.

3. Skim the excess fat from the juices, then return the chicken to the slow cooker. Turn the setting to high.

4. Bring a large saucepan of lightly salted water to a boil. Add the pasta, bring back to a boil, and cook according to the package directions until tender but still firm to the bite. Drain, add to the chicken, and stir well.

5. Stir the tagliatelle and dill into the slow cooker, cover, and cook on high for an additional 20 minutes. Garnish with extra dill and serve immediately.

CHICKEN TORTILLA SOUP

serves **4–6**

1 tablespoon vegetable oil
1 onion, diced
1 teaspoon chili powder
1 teaspoon salt
½ teaspoon ground cumin
2 tablespoons tomato paste
3½ cups chicken stock
1 (14½-ounce) can diced tomatoes,
 with juice
1 green chile, cored, seeded, and
 finely chopped
1 pound bone-in, skinless
 chicken thighs
1½ cups small tortilla chip pieces,
plus extra to serve

To serve
1 ripe avocado, diced
chopped fresh cilantro
1 lime, cut into wedges

This healthy soup is a hearty first course or a light meal in a bowl.

1. Heat the oil in a large skillet over medium–high heat. Add the onion and cook, stirring occasionally, for about 5 minutes, until soft. Add the chili powder, salt, cumin, and tomato paste and cook, stirring, for an additional 1 minute. Add one-third of the stock to the skillet and bring to a boil, stirring and scraping up any brown sediment on the bottom of the skillet.

2. Transfer the mixture to the slow cooker. Add the remaining stock, the tomatoes, chile, chicken, and tortilla chips, then cover and cook on low for about 4 hours or on high for 8 hours, until the chicken is cooked through and tender.

3. Lift out the chicken using a slotted spoon, remove and discard the bones, and shred the meat. Return the chicken to the slow cooker, cover, and heat on high for about 5 minutes, until heated through. Serve hot, accompanied by diced avocado, chopped cilantro, lime wedges, and tortilla chips.

NEW ENGLAND CLAM CHOWDER

serves **4**

2 tablespoons butter
1 onion, finely chopped
2 potatoes, cut into cubes
1 large carrot, diced
1¾ cups fish stock or water
1 (10-ounce) can clams, drained
1 cup heavy cream
salt and pepper, to taste
chopped fresh parsley, to garnish
fresh crusty bread, to serve

Many recipes for this fish soup exist up and down the east coast — some have a creamy consistency, while others use tomatoes for color and flavor.

1. Melt the butter in a skillet, add the onion, and sauté over medium heat for 4–5 minutes, stirring, until golden.

2. Transfer the onion to the slow cooker with the potatoes, carrot, and stock and season with salt and pepper. Cover and cook on high for 3 hours.

3. Add the clams and the cream to the slow cooker and stir to mix evenly. Cover and cook for an additional 1 hour.

4. Adjust the seasoning. Transfer to warm serving bowls, sprinkle with parsley, and serve immediately with crusty bread.

SHRIMP BISQUE

serves **4–6**

1 tablespoon butter
1 onion, diced
½ cup long-grain rice
2 tablespoons tomato paste
1½ teaspoons salt
½ teaspoon cayenne pepper
8½ cups low-sodium shrimp
   stock or fish stock
1 carrot, diced
1 celery stalk, diced
3 cups diced button mushrooms
1½ pounds raw shrimp, shelled,
   deveined, and cut into bite-size
   pieces, if large
⅔ cup heavy cream
2 tablespoons lemon juice
snipped chives, to garnish

Thickened with rice, this decadent seafood soup tastes delicious and is also a healthy option.

1. Melt the butter in a large skillet over medium–high heat. Add the onion and cook, stirring, for about 5 minutes, until soft. Add the rice, tomato paste, salt, and cayenne pepper and cook, stirring, for an additional 1 minute. Add one-quarter of the stock and cook, stirring, for about 1 minute, scraping up any sediment from the bottom of the skillet.

2. Add the onion mixture to the slow cooker together with the carrot, celery, mushrooms, and remaining stock. Cover and cook on high for 3 hours or on low for 6 hours.

3. Using a food processor or blender, puree the soup in batches. Return to the slow cooker, add the shrimp, cover, and cook on high for 30 minutes, until the shrimp are cooked through. Stir in the cream and lemon juice and serve hot, garnished with the chives.

SALMON CHOWDER

serves **4**

1 tablespoon butter
1 tablespoon sunflower oil
1 onion, finely chopped
1 leek, finely chopped
1 fennel bulb, finely chopped,
  feathery tops reserved
2 cups diced Yukon gold
  or white round potatoes
3 cups fish stock
1 pound salmon fillet, skinned and
  cut into cubes
1¼ cups milk
⅔ cup light cream
2 tablespoons chopped fresh dill
salt and pepper, to taste

Salmon and fennel are the perfect match in this recipe, which makes a great appetizer for a special dinner. For a family supper, the salmon could be replaced by any firm white fish you choose.

1. Melt the butter with the oil in a saucepan. Add the onion, leek, and fennel and cook over low heat, stirring occasionally, for 5 minutes. Add the potatoes and cook, stirring occasionally, for an additional 4 minutes, then pour in the stock and season with salt and pepper. Bring to a boil, then transfer to the slow cooker. Cover and cook on low for 3 hours, until the potatoes are tender.

2. Meanwhile, chop the fennel fronds and set aside. Add the salmon to the slow cooker, pour in the milk and stir gently. Replace the lid and cook on low for 30 minutes, until the fish flakes easily.

3. Gently stir in the cream, dill, and the reserved fennel fronds, replace the lid, and cook for an additional 10–15 minutes, until heated through. Taste and adjust the seasoning, adding salt and pepper, if needed. Serve immediately.

VIETNAMESE BEEF NOODLE SOUP

serves **4**

8½ cups beef stock

1 onion, quartered

2-inch piece of fresh ginger,
  thickly sliced lengthwise

2 cinnamon sticks

3 whole cloves

2 star anise or 1 teaspoon fennel seeds

2 tablespoons Thai fish sauce

1 teaspoon sugar

1 pound dried rice noodles

8 ounces top sirloin steak,
  very thinly sliced

salt, to taste

Accompaniments, to serve

1 cup bean sprouts

lime wedges

chopped fresh herbs, including basil,
  cilantro and/or mint

4 scallions, thinly sliced

2 hot chiles, thinly sliced

You'll find it easier to cut the very thin slices of steak needed for this dish if you freeze the meat for 15 minutes before slicing.

1. Put the stock, onion, ginger, cinnamon sticks, cloves, star anise, fish sauce, and sugar into the slow cooker and stir to combine. Cover and cook on high for 5 hours or on low for 8 hours. Season with salt.

2. Pour the liquid through a fine-mesh strainer or a colander lined with cheesecloth and discard the solids. Return the clear stock to the slow cooker and heat on high for about 30 minutes, until hot, or transfer to a large saucepan and bring to a slow boil over medium–high heat.

3. Just before serving, cook the noodles according to the package instructions.

4. Put a few slices of beef into the bottom of each of four soup bowls and ladle the soup over the top to lightly cook the beef. Add some noodles to each bowl. Serve immediately with the accompaniments set out in small bowls for the diners to help themselves.

TOMATO & LENTIL SOUP

serves **4**

2 tablespoons sunflower oil
1 onion, chopped
1 garlic clove, finely chopped
2 celery stalks, chopped
2 carrots, chopped
1 teaspoon ground cumin
1 teaspoon ground coriander
1 cup red or yellow lentils
1 tablespoon tomato paste
5 cups vegetable stock
1 (14½-ounce) can diced tomatoes
1 bay leaf
salt and pepper, to taste
crème fraîche or sour cream and
  toasted crusty bread, to serve

Simple yet satisfying and flavored with the warm spices of cumin and coriander, basic lentils can be easily transformed into a healthy bowl of soup.

1. Heat the oil in a saucepan. Add the onion and garlic and cook over low heat, stirring occasionally, for 5 minutes, until softened. Stir in the celery and carrots and cook, stirring occasionally, for an additional 4 minutes. Stir in the ground cumin and coriander and cook, stirring, for 1 minute, then add the lentils.

2. Mix the tomato paste with a little of the stock in a small bowl and add to the pan with the remaining stock, the tomatoes, and bay leaf. Bring to a boil, then transfer to the slow cooker. Stir well, cover, and cook on low for 3½–4 hours.

3. Remove and discard the bay leaf. Transfer the soup to a food processor or blender and process until smooth. Season with salt and pepper. Ladle into warm soup bowls, top each with a dollop of crème fraîche, and serve immediately with toasted crusty bread.

ITALIAN BREAD SOUP WITH GREENS

serves **4**

2 tablespoons olive oil

1 onion, diced

1 leek, halved lengthwise and
    thinly sliced

5 cups vegetable stock

3 cups chopped kale

2 celery stalks, diced

2 carrots, diced

1 teaspoon crumbled dried oregano

1½ teaspoons salt

½ teaspoon pepper

7 slices day-old sourdough bread, cubed

⅓ cup freshly grated Parmesan cheese,
    to garnish

Turn this healthy, vegetable-packed soup into a one-dish meal by adding a can of cannellini beans along with the vegetables.

1. Heat the oil in a large skillet over medium–high heat. Add the onion and leek and sauté for about 5 minutes, until soft.

2. Transfer the mixture to the slow cooker and add the stock, kale, celery, carrots, and oregano and season with salt and pepper. Cover and cook on high for about 4 hours or on low for 8 hours.

3. Add the bread to the soup, cover, and cook on high, stirring occasionally, for about 30 minutes, until the bread breaks down and thickens the soup.

4. Serve hot, garnished with the cheese.

GREEK BEAN & VEGETABLE SOUP

serves **4—6**

2½ cups dried navy beans,
  soaked in cold water overnight
  (or at least 5 hours)
2 onions, finely chopped
2 garlic cloves, finely chopped
2 potatoes, chopped
2 carrots, chopped
2 tomatoes, peeled and chopped
2 celery stalks, chopped
¼ cup extra-virgin olive oil
1 bay leaf
salt and pepper, to taste
12 black olives and 2 tablespoons
  snipped chives, to garnish

A wonderful recipe when you need something simple and nutritious that requires little preparation. This soup is a great choice for vegetarians, too.

1. Drain the beans and rinse well under cold running water. Put the beans into a saucepan, cover with fresh cold water, and bring to a boil. Boil rapidly for at least 10 minutes, then remove from the heat and drain and rinse again.

2. Put the beans into the slow cooker and add the onions, garlic, potatoes, carrots, tomatoes, celery, olive oil, and bay leaf.

3. Pour in 8½ cups boiling water, making sure that all the ingredients are fully submerged. Cover and cook on low for 12 hours, until the beans are tender.

4. Remove and discard the bay leaf. Season the soup with salt and pepper and garnish with the olives and chives. Transfer into warm soup bowls and serve.

TUSCAN WHITE BEAN SPREAD WITH ROASTED GARLIC

serves **6—8**

1 garlic bulb

3 tablespoons olive oil

1 (15-ounce) can cannellini beans,
  rinsed and drained

2 tablespoons lemon juice

2 teaspoons finely chopped
  fresh rosemary

1/8–1/4 teaspoon cayenne pepper,
  plus extra to taste

1 cup freshly grated
  Parmesan cheese

salt, to taste

baguette slices, to serve

Slow cooking is an easy way to roast garlic, giving it an enticing mellow and savory caramelized flavor, without having to tend it while it cooks.

1. Keeping the garlic bulb intact, slice about ½ inch off the top, exposing the cloves. Fill the slow cooker with water to a depth of about ¼ inch. Stand the garlic bulb cut-side up in the slow cooker and drizzle 1 tablespoon of the oil over the top. Cover and cook on low for about 6 hours, until the garlic is soft and golden brown. Remove the garlic, let cool, then squeeze the cloves into a small bowl.

2. Put the beans, half of the roasted garlic (reserve the remaining garlic for another recipe), lemon juice, rosemary, cayenne pepper, and ¼ teaspoon of salt into a food processor and process until smooth.

3. Add the cheese and pulse until well-combined. If the mixture is too thick, add 1–2 tablespoons of water and pulse to incorporate. Taste and add more salt and cayenne pepper, if necessary. Serve with baguette slices.

WARM CHICKPEA SALAD

serves **6**

1¼ cups dried chickpeas,
  soaked overnight in cold
  water and drained
1 cup pitted black olives
4 scallions, finely chopped
fresh parsley sprigs, to garnish
crusty bread, to serve

Dressing
2 tablespoons red-wine vinegar
2 tablespoons mixed chopped fresh
  herbs, such as parsley, rosemary,
  and thyme
3 garlic cloves, minced
½ cup extra-virgin olive oil
salt and pepper, to taste

A great appetizer served warm, but equally tasty if you chill it and serve cold. As a variation, you could add flaked, canned tuna and serve piled in baked potatoes.

1. Put the chickpeas into the slow cooker and add enough boiling water to cover. Cover and cook on low for 12 hours.

2. Drain well and transfer to a bowl. Stir in the olives and scallions.

3. To make the dressing, whisk together the vinegar, herbs, and garlic in a small bowl and season with salt and pepper. Gradually whisk in the olive oil. Pour the dressing over the still-warm chickpeas and toss lightly to coat. Garnish with the parsley sprigs and serve warm with crusty bread.

PEARS STUFFED WITH BLUE CHEESE

serves **4**

2 just-ripe pears
1 cup crumbled Gorgonzola cheese
   or other blue cheese
1 tablespoon honey
¼ cup chopped pecans or walnuts

Use spiced, candied nuts instead of plain chopped nuts for a sophisticated touch.

1. Fill the slow cooker with water to a depth of about 1 inch.

2. Halve the pears lengthwise and scoop out the cores. Slice off a part from the outside of each pear half to make a flat surface, so that the pears will sit level when placed in the slow cooker.

3. Divide the cheese equally among the pear halves, pressing it into the hollows. Place the pears, cheese-side up, in the slow cooker in a single layer and drizzle the honey evenly over the top. Cover and cook on high for about 2 hours, until the pears are soft.

4. Remove the pears from the slow cooker with a slotted spoon and arrange on a serving plate. Sprinkle the nuts evenly over the pears. If liked, brown the pears under the broiler for 1–2 minutes. Serve hot.

STUFFED CABBAGE ROLLS

serves **6**

2 cups mixed nuts, finely ground
2 onions, finely chopped
1 garlic clove, finely chopped
2 celery stalks, finely chopped
1 cup shredded cheddar cheese
1 teaspoon finely chopped fresh thyme
2 eggs
1 teaspoon yeast extract
12 large green cabbage leaves

Tomato sauce
2 tablespoons sunflower oil
2 onions, chopped
2 garlic cloves, finely chopped
2½ cups canned diced tomatoes
2 tablespoons tomato paste
1½ teaspoons sugar
1 bay leaf
salt and pepper, to taste

1. To make the tomato sauce, heat the oil in a heavy saucepan. Add the onions and cook over medium heat, stirring occasionally, for 5 minutes, until softened. Stir in the garlic and cook for 1 minute, then add the tomatoes, tomato paste, sugar, and bay leaf. Season with salt and pepper and bring to a boil. Reduce the heat and simmer gently for 20 minutes, until thickened.

2. Meanwhile, mix together the nuts, onions, garlic, celery, cheese, and thyme in a bowl. Lightly beat the eggs with the yeast extract in a small bowl, then stir into the nut mixture. Set aside.

3. Cut out the thick stem from the cabbage leaves. Blanch the leaves in a large saucepan of boiling water for 5 minutes, then drain and refresh under cold water. Pat dry with paper towels.

4. Place a little of the nut mixture on the stem end of each cabbage leaf. Fold the sides over, then roll up to make a neat package.

5. Arrange the packages in the slow cooker, seam-side down. Remove and discard the bay leaf from the tomato sauce and pour the sauce over the cabbage rolls. Cover and cook on low for 3–4 hours. Serve the cabbage rolls hot or cold.

STUFFED CHILE PEPPERS

serves **4**

4 large poblano or pasilla chiles
1 tablespoon vegetable oil
1 onion, diced
1 pound fresh ground turkey
1 teaspoon ground cumin
1 teaspoon mild chili powder
1 teaspoon crumbled dried oregano
1 teaspoon salt
1 cup salsa, hot or mild, to taste
1 cup shredded sharp cheddar cheese
4 extra-large eggs, lightly beaten
2 tablespoons all-purpose flour
¾ cup canned evaporated milk

This flavorsome dish is an easy and healthy version of the traditional Mexican specialty, chile rellenos.

1. Preheat the broiler to high. Put the chiles on a baking sheet, put under the preheated broiler, and cook for 3–5 minutes on each side, until the skin begins to blister and blacken. Remove from the broiler, put into a bowl, and cover with plastic wrap. Let steam for about 10 minutes, until cool enough to handle, then peel off the skins. Make a slit down one side of each chile to open it up and remove the stem and seeds.

2. Heat the oil in a large skillet over medium–high heat. Add the onion and cook, stirring, for about 5 minutes, until soft. Add the turkey and cook, breaking up the meat with a wooden spoon, for about 4 minutes, or until brown. Stir in the cumin, chili powder, oregano, and salt and cook for an additional 1 minute. Stir in the salsa and three-quarters of the cheese.

3. Lay the chiles, cut-side up, on a work surface. Stuff them with the turkey mixture, dividing the mixture equally among them. Place the stuffed chiles in the slow cooker in a single layer.

4. Put the eggs, flour, and evaporated milk into a mixing bowl and whisk together. Pour the egg mixture over the chiles and top with the remaining cheese. Cover and cook on low for 2 hours, until puffed and golden brown. Serve hot.

SWEET & SOUR CHICKEN WINGS

serves **4–6**

2¼ pounds chicken wings, tips removed

2 celery stalks, chopped

3 cups hot chicken stock

2 tablespoons cornstarch

3 tablespoons white-wine vinegar
  or rice vinegar

3 tablespoons dark soy sauce

⅓ cup sweet chili sauce

¼ cup firmly packed light brown sugar

2 cups drained canned pineapple
  chunks in juice

1 (8-ounce) can sliced bamboo shoots,
  drained and rinsed

½ green bell pepper, seeded and
  thinly sliced

½ red bell pepper, seeded and
  thinly sliced

salt, to taste

steamed bok choy, to serve

1. Put the chicken wings and celery in the slow cooker and season well with salt. Pour in the stock, cover, and cook on low for 5 hours.

2. Drain the chicken wings, reserving 1½ cups of the stock, and keep warm. Pour the reserved stock into a saucepan and stir in the cornstarch. Add the vinegar, soy sauce, and chili sauce. Put over medium heat and stir in the sugar. Cook, stirring continuously, for 5 minutes, or until the sugar has dissolved completely and the sauce is thickened, smooth, and clear.

3. Reduce the heat, stir in the pineapple, bamboo shoots, and bell peppers, and simmer gently for 2–3 minutes. Stir in the chicken wings until they are thoroughly coated, then transfer to warm serving bowls. Serve immediately with bok choy.

SPICY CHICKEN & CHEESE DIP

serves **6–8**

4 cups shredded Gouda cheese
2 cups diced cooked chicken breast
1 cup chunky salsa, hot or mild
1 cup sour cream
3 scallions, thinly sliced, to garnish
chopped fresh cilantro, to garnish
tortilla chips, to serve

This spicy dip will get any fiesta off to a great start. Use spicy salsa if you like a kick, or keep it tame with a milder version.

1. Put the cheese, chicken, and salsa into the slow cooker, stir to mix well, cover, and cook on low for 2 hours.

2. Stir in the sour cream, replace the lid, and cook on high for an additional 20 minutes, until heated through.

3. Serve hot, garnished with the scallions and cilantro, with tortilla chips for dipping.

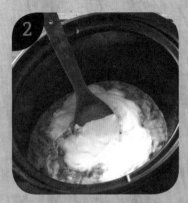

CHICKEN QUESADILLAS

serves **4**

4 skinless, boneless chicken breasts

½ teaspoon crushed dried chiles

2 garlic cloves, crushed

2 tablespoons finely chopped parsley

2 tablespoons olive oil

2½ cups cherry tomatoes

4 large wheat tortillas

8 ounces mozzarella cheese

salt and pepper, to taste

Quesadillas are toasted tortilla wraps with cheese inside. You can create many delicious fillings, including this spicy marinated chicken mix.

1. Put the chicken into a bowl with the chiles, garlic, parsley, and 1 tablespoon olive oil, and turn to coat evenly. Cover and let sit in the refrigerator to marinate for at least 1 hour, or overnight.

2. Transfer the tomatoes to the slow cooker and arrange the chicken breasts on top. Season with salt and pepper. Cover and cook on high for 2 hours, until tender.

3. Remove the chicken and shred the meat, using two forks. Place on one side of each tortilla and top with the tomatoes. Chop or tear the mozzarella and arrange on top. Moisten the edges of the tortillas and fold over to enclose the filling.

4. Brush a ridged grill pan or large skillet with the remaining oil and put over medium heat. Add the quesadillas to the pan and cook until golden, turning once. Cut into wedges and serve. Any spare juices can be spooned over the top.

MANGO BEEF IN LETTUCE CUPS

serves **6–8**

1½ pounds chuck steak,
  cut into ½-inch dice
1 tablespoon cornstarch
1 fresh mango, peeled, pitted, and diced
2 hot red chiles, cored and diced
2 tablespoons soy sauce
2 tablespoons mirin or other
  sweet white wine
2 tablespoons packed light brown sugar
1 teaspoon sesame oil
cup-shape lettuce leaves, to serve

This unusual appetizer offers a tantalizing combination of sweet and spicy flavors.

1. Put the beef and the cornstarch into the slow cooker and toss to coat the beef evenly. Add the mango and chiles and stir to mix. Add the soy sauce, mirin, sugar, and oil and stir to mix well.

2. Cover and cook on high for about 1 hour, then set the lid slightly ajar and continue to cook on high for an additional 1 hour, until the meat is tender and the sauce has thickened.

3. Transfer the meat to a serving bowl and serve with the lettuce leaves, so that diners can scoop some of the meat into a lettuce cup and wrap it up like a taco.

BEEF & CHIPOTLE BURRITOS

serves **4**

1 tablespoon olive oil
1 onion, sliced
1¼ pounds steak
1 dried chipotle pepper, soaked in
  boiling water for 20 minutes
1 garlic clove, crushed
1 teaspoon ground cumin
1 (14-ounce) can diced tomatoes
8 large tortillas
salt and pepper, to taste
sour cream and green salad, to serve

Chipotle peppers are smoked, dried, jalapeño chiles, which have been used in Mexican cooking for centuries. In this recipe, they add the heat to a spicy beef filling for tortillas.

1. Heat the olive oil in a saucepan and sauté the onion for 3–4 minutes, until golden. Transfer to the slow cooker and arrange the beef on top. Drain and chop the chipotle. Sprinkle the garlic, cumin, and tomatoes over the meat and season with salt and pepper.

2. Cover and cook on low for 4 hours, until the meat is tender.

3. Warm the tortillas. Remove the beef and shred with a fork. Divide among the tortillas and spoon the sauce over the top. Wrap, and serve with sour cream and green salad.

BEEF EMPANADAS

makes about **30**

1 tablespoon vegetable oil

1 onion, finely chopped

1 garlic clove, finely chopped

1 pound extra-lean fresh ground beef

1 teaspoon salt

1 teaspoon ground cumin

1 teaspoon chili powder

1 teaspoon dried oregano or
  1 tablespoon finely chopped
  fresh oregano

1 red bell pepper, cored, seeded,
  and diced

¾ cup pimiento-stuffed green olives,
  chopped

¼ cup golden raisins

2 tablespoons tomato paste

1 (15-ounce) package rolled dough
  pie crust, thawed if frozen

flour, for dusting

These tempting bites are always a hit at parties. Freeze a batch before baking, and be ready for a fiesta at a moment's notice.

1. Heat the oil in a large skillet over medium–high heat. Add the onion and garlic and cook, stirring, for about 5 minutes, until soft. Add the beef and cook, stirring, until brown. Drain off the excess fat and discard. Add the salt, cumin, chili powder, and oregano and continue to cook, stirring, for an additional minute, then transfer to the slow cooker.

2. Add the red bell pepper, olives, golden raisins, and tomato paste and stir to combine. Cover and cook on low for 4 hours.

3. Preheat the oven to 400°F and line a baking sheet with parchment paper. Roll out the dough on a lightly floured surface and cut it into 2½-inch circles with a pastry cutter. Place about 1 tablespoon of the filling on each circle, fold over the dough, and crimp together the edges to seal each pie.

4. Place the finished empanadas on the prepared baking sheet and bake in the preheated oven for 20–25 minutes, until golden brown. Remove from the oven and transfer to a wire rack to cool slightly. Serve warm.

CHAPTER 2
EVERYDAY EATING

Chicken & Apple Stew 57

Chicken with Olives & Sun-Dried Tomatoes 58

Chicken & Mushroom Stew 60

Chicken Paprika 62

Easy Chinese Chicken 65

Turkey Chili with Sweet Potatoes 66

Turkey Hash 69

Chinese Barbecue Pork 70

Spicy Pulled Pork 73

Korean Braised Beef Short Ribs 74

Chunky Beef Chili 77

Beef Gyros with Yogurt Sauce 78

Beef Ragu with Tagliatelle 81

Moroccan Beef Stew 82

Classic Pot Roast 85

Thai Beef Curry 86

Steamed Fish with Ginger, Tomatoes & Beans 88

Jambalaya 91

Salmon with Leeks & Cream 92

Tagliatelle with Tuna 95

CHICKEN & APPLE STEW

serves **4**

1 tablespoon olive oil

4 chicken parts (about 6 ounces each)

1 onion, chopped

2 celery stalks, coarsely chopped

1$\frac{1}{2}$ tablespoons all-purpose flour

1$\frac{1}{4}$ cups apple juice

$\frac{2}{3}$ cup chicken stock

1 Granny Smith apple or other cooking
  apple, cored and cut into quarters

2 bay leaves

1–2 teaspoons honey

1 yellow bell pepper, seeded and
  cut into chunks

salt and pepper, to taste

To garnish

1 large or 2 medium, Gala, Golden
  Delicious, or Cortland apples,
  cored and sliced

1 tablespoon butter, melted

2 tablespoons raw brown sugar

1 tablespoon chopped fresh mint

Chicken and apples go together so well. In this recipe, the soft apple cooked with the chicken adds sharpness, while the garnish of caramelized apples provides sweetness and crunch.

1. Heat the oil in a heavy skillet. Add the chicken and cook over medium–high heat, turning frequently, for 10 minutes, until golden brown. Transfer to the slow cooker. Add the onion and celery to the skillet and cook over low heat for 5 minutes, until softened. Sprinkle in the flour and cook for 2 minutes, then remove the skillet from the heat.

2. Gradually stir in the apple juice and stock, then return the skillet to the heat and bring to a boil. Stir in the Granny Smith apple, bay leaves, and honey and season with salt and pepper. Pour the mixture over the chicken in the slow cooker, cover, and cook on low for 6$\frac{1}{2}$ hours, until the chicken is tender and cooked through. Stir in the bell pepper, replace the lid, and cook on high for 45 minutes.

3. Shortly before serving, preheat the broiler. Brush one side of the apple slices with half the melted butter and sprinkle with half the sugar. Cook under the preheated broiler for 2–3 minutes, until the sugar has caramelized. Turn the slices over with tongs, brush with the remaining butter, and sprinkle with the remaining sugar. Broil for an additional 2 minutes. Transfer the stew to warm plates and garnish with the caramelized apple slices and the mint. Serve immediately.

CHICKEN WITH OLIVES & SUN-DRIED TOMATOES

serves **4**

2 pounds skinless, bone-in chicken
 thighs, drumsticks, or a combination
1 teaspoon salt
½ teaspoon pepper
3 tablespoons all-purpose flour
2 tablespoons olive oil, plus extra
 if needed
1 onion, diced
3 garlic cloves, finely chopped
½ cup dry white wine
1 (28-ounce) can diced tomatoes
1 cup pitted Kalamata olives, quartered
1 cup chopped sun-dried tomatoes
fresh basil leaves, to garnish
cooked pasta, to serve

With easy preparation and a long cooking time, this chicken stew offers a taste of France with minimal effort.

1. Season the chicken with half the salt and all the pepper. Put the flour into a plastic food bag, add the chicken parts, in batches, if necessary, then hold the top securely closed and shake well to coat.

2. Heat the oil in a large skillet over medium–high heat. Add the chicken parts and cook on one side for about 4 minutes, until brown. Turn and cook on the other side for about 4 minutes, until brown. Put the chicken into the slow cooker.

3. Add some more oil to the skillet, if needed, then add the onion and garlic and sauté over medium heat for 15 minutes, until soft. Add the wine and bring to a boil. Cook, stirring and scraping up any sediment from the bottom of the skillet, for about 2 minutes. Add the canned tomatoes, olives, sun-dried tomatoes, and the remaining salt and cook, stirring, for about 1 minute.

4. Add the mixture to the slow cooker on top of the chicken. Cover and cook on high for 4 hours or on low for 8 hours. Serve hot with pasta, garnished with basil.

CHICKEN &
MUSHROOM STEW

serves **4**

1 tablespoon unsalted butter

2 tablespoons olive oil

4 pounds skinless chicken parts

2 red onions, sliced

2 garlic cloves, finely chopped

1 (14-ounce) can diced tomatoes

2 tablespoons chopped fresh
   flat-leaf parsley

6 fresh basil leaves, torn

1 tablespoon sun-dried tomato paste

²/₃ cup red wine

3 cups sliced mushrooms

salt and pepper, to taste

An ideal recipe for a family meal but also a great choice for a dinner with friends. Experiment with the wide variety of mushrooms available in your supermarket.

1. Heat the butter and oil in a heavy skillet. Add the chicken, in batches if necessary, and cook over medium–high heat, turning frequently, for 10 minutes, until golden brown all over. Using a slotted spoon, transfer the chicken to the slow cooker.

2. Add the onions and garlic to the skillet and cook over low heat, stirring occasionally, for 10 minutes, until golden. Add the tomatoes with their can juices, stir in the parsley, basil, tomato paste, and wine, and season with salt and pepper. Bring to a boil, then pour the mixture over the chicken.

3. Cover the slow cooker and cook on low for 6½ hours. Stir in the mushrooms, replace the lid, and cook on high for 30 minutes, until the chicken is tender and the vegetables are cooked through. Taste and adjust the seasoning, if necessary, and serve immediately.

CHICKEN PAPRIKA

serves **4**

2 pounds skinless, bone-in chicken
 thighs or drumsticks, or a combination
1 teaspoon salt
½ teaspoon pepper
⅔ cup all-purpose flour
2 tablespoons vegetable oil
1 tablespoon butter
1 large onion, diced
3 tablespoons paprika
2 tablespoons tomato paste
1 cup chicken stock
½ cup sour cream
finely chopped fresh dill, to garnish
cooked egg noodles or dumplings,
 to serve

This hearty chicken stew, brightened with paprika and enriched with sour cream, will warm you right through on a cold night.

1. Season the chicken with ½ teaspoon of salt and all of the pepper. Put the flour into a plastic food bag, add the chicken parts, in batches if necessary, then hold the top securely closed and shake well to coat.

2. Heat the oil in a large skillet over medium–high heat. Add the chicken parts and cook on one side for about 4 minutes, until brown. Turn and cook on the other side for about 4 minutes, until brown. Put the chicken into the slow cooker.

3. Add the butter to the skillet and heat over medium–high heat, until melted. Add the onion and cook, stirring occasionally, for about 5 minutes, until soft. Add the paprika, tomato paste, and the remaining salt, and cook, stirring, for about 1 minute.

4. Add the stock and bring to a boil, stirring and scraping up the sediment from the bottom of the skillet. Cook for about 1 minute, then pour the onion mixture into the slow cooker over the chicken. Cover and cook on high for 6 hours or on low for 9 hours.

5. Just before serving, stir in the sour cream. Garnish with dill and serve with noodles.

Everyday Eating 62

EASY CHINESE CHICKEN

serves **4**

2 teaspoons grated fresh ginger

4 garlic cloves, finely chopped

2 star anise or 1 teaspoon
  five-spice powder

²/₃ cup Chinese rice wine or
  medium dry sherry

2 tablespoons dark soy sauce

1 teaspoon sesame oil

¹/₃ cup water

4 skinless chicken thighs or drumsticks

shredded scallions, to garnish

cooked rice, to serve

This great-tasting Chinese recipe can be served simply with steamed rice or as part of a more elaborate meal by adding a selection of quickly cooked stir-fried vegetables.

1. Mix together the ginger, garlic, star anise, rice wine, soy sauce, sesame oil, and water in a bowl. Put the chicken into a saucepan, add the spice mixture, and bring to a boil.

2. Transfer to the slow cooker, cover and cook on low for 4 hours, or until the chicken is tender and cooked through.

3. Remove and discard the star anise. Transfer the chicken to warm serving plates, garnish with shredded scallions, and serve immediately with rice.

TURKEY CHILI WITH SWEET POTATOES

serves **4–6**

1 tablespoon vegetable oil

1 onion, diced

1½ pounds fresh ground turkey

¼ cup tomato paste

1 tablespoon mild chili powder

1 teaspoon ground cumin

2 canned chipotle chiles in adobo sauce,
  seeded and diced, plus 2 teaspoons
  of the adobo sauce (or substitute
  1 teaspoon ground chipotles)

1 teaspoon salt

1 (14-ounce) can diced tomatoes

2 cups chicken stock

1 large sweet potato (about 8 ounces),
  diced

To serve

fresh cilantro

sour cream

shredded cheddar cheese

diced avocado

finely chopped red onion

Add a can of black beans along with the sweet potatoes to feed a crowd and make this healthy chili even better for you.

1. Heat the oil in a large skillet. Add the onion and cook, stirring, for about 5 minutes, until soft. Add the turkey and cook, breaking up the meat with a wooden spoon, for about 4 minutes, until brown. Stir in the tomato paste, chili powder, cumin, chiles and adobo sauce, and salt and cook for an additional 1 minute.

2. Transfer the mixture to the slow cooker. Stir in the tomatoes, stock, and sweet potato. Cover and cook on high for 4 hours or on low for 8 hours. Serve hot, accompanied by the cilantro, sour cream, cheese, avocado, and red onion.

TURKEY HASH

serves **4**

1 tablespoon olive oil

1 pound ground turkey

1 large red onion, diced

1/2 butternut squash, seeded,
  peeled, and diced

2 celery stalks, sliced

4 Yukon gold or white round potatoes,
  diced

3 tablespoons Worcestershire sauce

2 bay leaves

salt and pepper, to taste

This is a great-tasting combination because the slightly sweet, nutty flavor of the squash complements the rich turkey. Squash also keeps its shape well in the slow cooker.

1. Heat the oil in a skillet, add the turkey, and cook over high heat, stirring, until broken up and lightly browned.

2. Put all the vegetables into the slow cooker then add the turkey and pan juices. Add the Worcestershire sauce and bay leaves and season with salt and pepper. Cover and cook on low for 7 hours. Transfer to warm serving bowls and serve immediately.

CHINESE BARBECUE PORK

serves **4–6**

2 garlic cloves, finely chopped

1 tablespoon finely chopped fresh ginger

2 tablespoons honey

2 tablespoons soy sauce

2 tablespoons mirin or other
  sweet white wine

1 teaspoon sesame oil

1 teaspoon Chinese five-spice powder

2 pounds pork shoulder,
  boned and rolled

3 scallions, thinly sliced, to garnish

steamed rice, to serve

This easy, set-it-and-forget-it pork dish has all the typical flavors of slow-cooked Chinese pork.

1. Put the garlic, ginger, honey, soy sauce, mirin, oil, and five-spice powder into a large bowl and stir to mix. Add the pork and stir to coat. Cover and refrigerate for at least 2 hours or overnight.

2. Put the pork and the marinade into the slow cooker. Cover and cook on high for 6 hours or on low for 10 hours, until the meat is very tender.

3. Slice the meat and then pull into shreds using two forks. Garnish with scallions and serve hot with rice.

SPICY PULLED PORK

serves **4**

2 onions, sliced

3¼ pounds boned and rolled
   pork shoulder

2 tablespoons raw brown sugar

2 tablespoons Worcestershire sauce

1 tablespoon mustard

2 tablespoons ketchup

1 tablespoon cider vinegar

salt and pepper, to taste

hamburger buns or ciabatta rolls,
   to serve

Have your own hog roast at home! Slow cooking creates pork that's deliciously moist, tender, and full of flavor for the ultimate sandwich everyone will love.

1. Put the onions in the slow cooker and place the pork on top. Mix together the sugar, Worcestershire sauce, mustard, ketchup, and vinegar and spread all over the surface of the pork. Season with salt and pepper. Cover and cook on low for 8 hours.

2. Remove the pork from the slow cooker and use two forks to pull it apart into shreds.

3. Skim any excess fat from the juices and stir a little juice into the pork. Serve in hamburger buns, with the remaining juices for spooning over the top.

KOREAN BRAISED BEEF SHORT RIBS

serves **4–6**

1 onion, diced

3 garlic cloves, finely chopped

1 tablespoon finely chopped fresh ginger

2 tablespoons soy sauce

2 tablespoons packed dark brown sugar

2 tablespoons mirin or other
 sweet white wine

1 tablespoon sesame oil

1 teaspoon chili paste

3 pounds bone-in beef short ribs

2 small potatoes, cubed

2 carrots, cubed

3 scallions, thinly sliced, to garnish

1 tablespoon toasted sesame seeds,
 to garnish

steamed rice, to serve

If possible, ask your butcher to cut the ribs into 3-inch lengths to make serving easier.

1. Put the onion, garlic, ginger, soy sauce, sugar, mirin, oil, and chili paste into a bowl large enough to hold the meat and stir to combine. Add the ribs and turn to coat in the mixture. Cover and put into the refrigerator to marinate for at least 2 hours or overnight.

2. Put the beef, along with the marinade, into the slow cooker. Add the potatoes and carrots and stir to mix. Cover and cook on high for about 6 hours or on low for about 9 hours, until the meat is tender and falling off the bone.

3. Serve hot, garnished with the scallions and sesame seeds, with steamed rice.

CHUNKY BEEF CHILI

serves **4**

1⅓ cups dried red kidney beans,
 soaked overnight
2½ cups water
2 garlic cloves, chopped
⅓ cup tomato paste
1 small green chile, chopped
2 teaspoons ground cumin
2 teaspoons ground coriander
1¼ pounds chuck steak, diced
1 large onion, chopped
1 large green bell pepper, seeded
 and sliced
salt and pepper, to taste
sour cream, to serve

Chunks of beef, onions, garlic, and green bell pepper are cooked with chile to give just the right amount of kick. Serve with rice, tortilla chips, and guacamole for a satisfying meal.

1. Drain and rinse the beans, put into a saucepan, add enough water to cover, and bring to a boil. Boil rapidly for 10 minutes, then remove from the heat and drain and rinse again. Put the beans into the slow cooker and add the cold water.

2. Mix together the garlic, tomato paste, chile, cumin, and coriander in a large bowl. Add the steak, onion, and green bell pepper and mix to coat evenly.

3. Place the meat and vegetables on top of the beans, cover, and cook on low for 9 hours, until the beans and meat are tender. Stir and season with salt and pepper.

4. Transfer to warm serving bowls and top with a swirl of sour cream. Serve immediately.

BEEF GYROS WITH YOGURT SAUCE

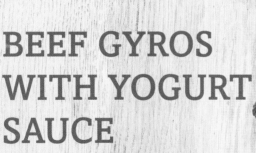

serves **4**

3 tablespoons plain yogurt

1 tablespoon lemon juice

2 garlic cloves, finely chopped

1 teaspoon crumbled dried oregano or
   1 tablespoon chopped fresh oregano

³/₄ teaspoon salt

¹/₂ teaspoon pepper

1¹/₂ pounds chuck steak, diced

Sauce

1 cucumber, peeled, seeded, and
   coarsely grated

1 teaspoon salt

1 cup plain yogurt

3 tablespoons lemon juice

1 cup chopped fresh mint leaves

To serve

4 warmed flatbreads or pita breads

1 large tomato, cut into wedges

2 cups shredded lettuce

Make this into a more traditionally Greek filling by using lamb instead of beef.

1. Put the yogurt, lemon juice, garlic, oregano, salt, and pepper into the slow cooker and stir to mix well. Add the beef and turn to coat. Cover and cook on high for about 5 hours or on low for about 9 hours, until the beef is tender. Shred the beef and mix it with the cooking juices.

2. To make the sauce, put the cucumber onto a double layer of paper towels and sprinkle with ¹/₂ teaspoon of the salt. Set aside. Put the yogurt, the remaining salt, lemon juice, and mint into medium bowl and stir to combine. Wrap the cucumber in the paper towels and squeeze out the excess juice over the sink. Mix the cucumber into the yogurt mixture.

3. Serve the shredded beef on flatbread, drizzled with the sauce and topped with tomato wedges and shredded lettuce.

BEEF RAGU WITH TAGLIATELLE

serves **6**

3 tablespoons olive oil

3 ounces pancetta or bacon, diced

1 onion, chopped

1 garlic clove, finely chopped

1 carrot, chopped

1 celery stalk, chopped

1 pound ground beef

½ cup red wine

2 tablespoons tomato paste

1 (14-ounce) can diced tomatoes

1¼ cups beef stock

½ teaspoon dried oregano

1 bay leaf

1 pound dried tagliatelle

salt and pepper, to taste

grated Parmesan cheese, to serve

This recipe may become your favorite accompaniment for simply cooked pasta. Long, slow cooking creates a rich-tasting sauce that coats and clings to the tagliatelle.

1. Heat the oil in a saucepan. Add the pancetta and cook over medium heat, stirring frequently, for 3 minutes. Reduce the heat, add the onion, garlic, carrot, and celery, and cook, stirring occasionally, for 5 minutes, until the vegetables have softened.

2. Increase the heat to medium and add the ground beef. Cook, stirring frequently and breaking it up with a wooden spoon, for 8–10 minutes, until evenly browned. Pour in the wine and cook for a few minutes, until the alcohol has evaporated, then stir in the tomato paste, tomatoes, stock, oregano, and bay leaf and season with salt and pepper.

3. Bring to a boil, then transfer the ragu sauce to the slow cooker. Cover and cook on low for 8–8½ hours.

4. Shortly before serving, bring a large saucepan of lightly salted water to a boil. Add the pasta, bring back to a boil, and cook according to the package directions until tender but still firm to the bite. Drain and transfer to a warm serving bowl. Remove and discard the bay leaf, then add the ragu sauce to the pasta. Toss with two forks, sprinkle with the Parmesan, and serve immediately.

MOROCCAN BEEF STEW

serves **4–6**

2 tablespoons vegetable oil
1 onion, diced
1¹⁄₂ teaspoons salt
¹⁄₂ teaspoon pepper
2 teaspoons ground cumin
¹⁄₂ teaspoon ground cinnamon
¹⁄₂ teaspoon ground ginger
1 cup red wine
1¹⁄₂ pounds chuck steak,
  cut into 2-inch pieces
1 cup diced dried apricots
2 tablespoons honey
¹⁄₂ cup water
chopped fresh cilantro, to garnish
cooked couscous, to serve

Heady spices and sweet dried apricots come together for an exotic twist on beef stew.

1. Heat the oil in a large skillet. Add the onion and cook, stirring, for about 5 minutes, until soft. Add the salt, pepper, cumin, cinnamon, and ginger and cook, stirring, for another 1 minute.

2. Add the wine, bring to a boil, and cook for 1 minute, scraping up any sediment from the bottom of the skillet. Transfer the mixture to the slow cooker.

3. Add the beef, apricots, honey, and water and stir to mix. Cover and cook on high for 6 hours or on low for 9 hours, until the meat is very tender.

4. Serve hot with couscous, garnished with cilantro.

CLASSIC POT ROAST

serves **6**

1 onion, finely chopped
4 carrots, sliced
4 baby turnips, sliced
4 celery stalks, sliced
2 potatoes, sliced
1 sweet potato, sliced
3–4 pounds bottom round or
  rump roast of beef, in one piece
1 bouquet garni (sprigs of parsley,
  bay leaf, and thyme tied together)
1¼ cups hot beef stock
salt and pepper, to taste

The ultimate one-pot roast that produces tender meat and perfectly cooked vegetables. The cooking juices can be thickened with cornstarch, if you prefer.

1. Put the onion, carrots, turnips, celery, potatoes, and sweet potato into the slow cooker and stir to mix well.

2. Rub the beef all over with salt and pepper, then place on top of the bed of vegetables. Add the bouquet garni and pour in the stock. Cover and cook on low for 9–10 hours, until the beef is cooked to your liking. Serve immediately.

THAI BEEF CURRY

serves **4**

¹⁄₃ cup Thai red curry paste

³⁄₄ cup coconut milk

¹⁄₄ cup firmly packed dark brown sugar

1 tablespoon Thai fish sauce

¹⁄₄ cup smooth peanut butter

2 pounds chuck steak,
  cut into 1-inch dice

2 potatoes, diced

¹⁄₂ cup beef stock or water

fresh basil leaves, cut into ribbons,
  to garnish

steamed rice, to serve

Enriched with coconut milk and peanut butter, this simple curry will transport you to Southeast Asia.

1. Put the curry paste, coconut milk, sugar, fish sauce, and peanut butter into the slow cooker and stir to combine. Add the beef, potatoes, and stock and stir to coat in the mixture.

2. Cover and cook on high for about 4 hours or on low for 8 hours, then set the lid slightly ajar and cook for an additional 1 hour, or until the beef is very tender and the sauce has thickened slightly. Serve hot, garnished with basil, with the steamed rice.

STEAMED FISH WITH GINGER, TOMATOES & BEANS

serves **4**

1 tablespoon finely chopped fresh ginger

2 garlic cloves, finely chopped

1–2 hot red chiles, cored, seeded, and diced

2 tablespoons Thai fish sauce

2 tablespoons mirin or other sweet white wine

1 teaspoon sugar

4 halibut fillets (about 1½ pounds in total)

vegetable oil, for oiling

3½ cups trimmed green beans

3 cups halved cherry tomatoes (or quartered if large)

To garnish

4 scallions, thinly sliced

finely chopped fresh cilantro

fresh basil leaves, shredded

This light and healthy main dish takes only minutes to prepare but is full of flavor.

1. Put the ginger, garlic, chiles, fish sauce, mirin, and sugar into a baking dish large enough to hold the fish and stir to combine. Add the fish and turn to coat in the mixture. Cover and put into the refrigerator to marinate for 30 minutes.

2. Meanwhile, brush four large square pieces of parchment paper with oil.

3. Divide the beans evenly among the prepared pieces of paper, piling them in the middle. Sprinkle the tomatoes evenly over them. Top each pile of vegetables with a fish fillet and some of the marinade. Fold up the packages securely, leaving a little room for the steam to circulate, and place them in the slow cooker. Cover and cook on high for about 2 hours, until the halibut is flaky and cooked through.

4. To serve, carefully remove the packages from the slow cooker, open them, and slide the contents onto warm plates, then garnish with scallions, cilantro, and basil.

JAMBALAYA

serves **4**

½ teaspoon cayenne pepper

2 teaspoons chopped fresh thyme

12 ounces skinless, boneless chicken
  breasts, diced

2 tablespoons vegetable oil

2 onions, chopped

2 garlic cloves, finely chopped

2 green bell peppers, seeded
  and chopped

2 celery stalks, chopped

4 ounces smoked ham, chopped

6 ounces chorizo sausage or other
  spicy sausage, sliced

1 (14-ounce) can diced tomatoes

2 tablespoons tomato paste

1 cup chicken stock

1 pound shrimp, peeled and deveined

3 cups cooked rice

salt and pepper

snipped fresh chives, to garnish

A great rice dish with a long history. Traditionally from Louisiana, it's also related to the Spanish national dish, paella, which uses a combination of chicken, spicy sausage, and shellfish.

1. Mix together the cayenne pepper, ½ teaspoon of pepper, 1 teaspoon of salt, and the thyme in a bowl. Add the chicken and toss to coat.

2. Heat the oil in a large, heavy saucepan. Add the onions, garlic, green bell peppers, and celery and cook over low heat, stirring occasionally, for 5 minutes. Add the chicken and cook over medium heat, stirring frequently, for an additional 5 minutes, until golden all over. Stir in the ham, chorizo, tomatoes, tomato paste, and stock and bring to a boil.

3. Transfer the mixture to the slow cooker. Cover and cook on low for 6 hours. Add the shrimp and rice, replace the lid, and cook on high for 30 minutes.

4. Taste and adjust the seasoning, adding salt and pepper, if necessary. Transfer to warm plates, garnish with chives, and serve immediately.

SALMON WITH LEEKS & CREAM

serves **4**

vegetable oil, for oiling
2 tablespoons butter
2 leeks, white and light green parts
  halved lengthwise, then thinly
  sliced crosswise
¼ cup dry white wine
½ cup heavy cream
1 teaspoon salt
½ teaspoon pepper
4 salmon fillets (about 6 ounces each)
8 small fresh sage leaves

This simple salmon dish makes an elegant meal.

1. Lightly brush four large square pieces of parchment paper with oil.

2. Heat the butter in a large skillet over medium–high heat, until melted and bubbling. Add the leeks and cook, stirring occasionally, for about 5 minutes, until soft.

3. Stir in the wine and bring to a boil. Cook, stirring and scraping up any sediment from the bottom of the skillet, for an additional 3 minutes, or until most of the wine has evaporated. Stir in the cream, salt, and pepper and cook, stirring, for about 2 minutes, until the cream is beginning to thicken.

4. Place one salmon fillet in the center of each prepared piece of paper. Top with the leek and cream mixture, then place two sage leaves on top of each portion. Fold up the packages securely, leaving a little room for the steam to circulate, then place them in the slow cooker. Cover and cook on high for about 2 hours, until the salmon is cooked through.

5. To serve, carefully remove the packages from the slow cooker, open them, and slide the contents onto warm plates. Serve immediately.

TAGLIATELLE WITH TUNA

serves **4**

8 ounces dried egg tagliatelle

1 (12-ounce) can solid white tuna in oil, drained

1 bunch scallions, sliced

1 cup frozen peas

2 teaspoon hot chili sauce

2½ cups hot chicken stock

1 cup shredded cheddar cheese

salt and pepper, to taste

When you just want a simple and tasty meal, this is the perfect choice. Serve with some crusty bread, a crisp salad, and perhaps a glass of white wine.

1. Bring a large saucepan of lightly salted water to a boil. Add the pasta, return to a boil, and cook for 2 minutes, until the pasta ribbons are loose. Drain.

2. Break up the tuna into bite-size chunks and put into the slow cooker with the pasta, scallions, and peas. Season with salt and pepper.

3. Add the chilli sauce to the stock and pour the liquid over the ingredients in the slow cooker. Sprinkle the shredded cheese over the top. Cover and cook on low for 2 hours. Serve immediately on warm plates.

CHAPTER 3
EASY ENTERTAINING

Chicken in Wine 99

Chicken Pot Pies 100

Chipotle Chicken Stew 103

Chicken Breasts Stuffed with Herbed Goat Cheese 104

Turkey & Rice Casserole 107

Turkey Breast with Bacon, Leeks & Prunes 108

Sausage & Bean Casserole 110

Pork Chops Stuffed with Apples 112

Ham Cooked in Cider 115

Beef Short Ribs Braised in Red Wine 116

Pot Roast with Beer 119

Steak Roll Ups with Spinach & Feta Cheese 120

Lamb Shanks with Olives 122

Honey-Glazed Duck Legs 124

Seafood Stew 127

Easy Bouillabaisse with Garlic Mayonnaise 128

Salmon with Dill & Lime 131

Clams in Spicy Broth 132

Sea Bream in Lemon Sauce 135

Halibut with Fennel & Olives 136

CHICKEN IN WINE

serves **4–6**

2 tablespoons all-purpose flour
1 (3¹/₂ -pound) chicken, cut into 8 parts
4 tablespoons unsalted butter
1 tablespoon sunflower oil
4 shallots, finely chopped
12 button mushrooms, sliced
2 tablespoons brandy
2 cups dry white wine
1 cup heavy cream
salt and pepper, to taste
cooked green vegetables,
 to serve

1. Put the flour into a plastic food bag and season with salt and pepper. Add the chicken parts, in batches, hold the top securely, and shake well to coat. Transfer the chicken to a plate.

2. Heat half the butter with the oil in a heavy skillet. Add the chicken parts and cook over medium–high heat, turning frequently, for 10 minutes, until golden all over. Using a slotted spoon, transfer them to a plate.

3. Wipe out the skillet with paper towels, then return to medium–high heat and melt the remaining butter. Add the shallots and mushrooms and cook, stirring continuously, for 3 minutes. Return the chicken to the skillet and remove it from the heat. Warm the brandy in a small ladle, ignite, and pour it over the chicken, shaking the skillet gently until the flames die down.

4. Return the skillet to the heat and pour in the wine. Bring to a boil over low heat, scraping up any sediment from the bottom of the skillet. Transfer to the slow cooker, cover, and cook on low for 5–6 hours, until the chicken is tender and cooked through.

5. Transfer the chicken to a serving dish and keep warm. Skim off any fat from the surface of the cooking liquid and pour the liquid into a saucepan. Stir in the cream and bring just to a boil over low heat, then pour the sauce over the chicken. Serve immediately with green vegetables.

CHICKEN POT PIES

serves **6**

3 tablespoons butter

1 onion, diced

2 cups diced button mushrooms

1½ pounds boneless,
  skinless chicken, diced

1 carrot, diced

2 celery stalks, diced

1 tablespoon fresh thyme leaves

2 tablespoons all-purpose flour

1 cup milk

¾ cup chicken stock

1 teaspoon salt

½ teaspoon pepper

2 sheets ready-to-bake puff pastry

flour, for dusting

1. Melt 1 tablespoon of the butter in a large skillet over medium–high heat. Add the onion and cook, stirring, for about 5 minutes, until soft. Add the mushrooms and cook, stirring, for an additional 3 minutes, or until the mushrooms are beginning to soften. Transfer the mixture to the slow cooker and add the chicken, carrot, celery, and thyme.

2. Reduce the heat under the skillet to medium, add the remaining butter, and heat until melted. Whisk in the flour and cook, whisking continuously, until the mixture is lightly browned and begins to release a nutty aroma. Whisk in the milk, stock, salt, and pepper and continue to cook, stirring, for an additional 5 minutes, or until the mixture begins to thicken.

3. Add the mixture to the slow cooker and stir to mix well. Cover and cook on high for about 4 hours or on low for about 8 hours, until the chicken is tender and sauce has thickened. Divide the filling equally among six 1-cup ramekins.

4. Preheat the oven to 375°F. Roll out the dough on a lightly floured surface and cut out six circles, each about 1 inch larger in circumference than the ramekins. Top each filled ramekin with a dough circle, crimping the edges. Prick the dough on each pie several times with a fork.

5. Place the ramekins on a baking sheet and bake in the preheated oven for about 20 minutes, until the pastry is puffed and golden brown. Let cool for about 10 minutes before serving.

CHIPOTLE CHICKEN STEW

serves **4–6**

1 cup dried navy beans,
  soaked overnight
1 large onion, sliced
1 dried chipotle pepper, soaked for
  20 minutes, then drained and
  finely chopped
1 (3¼-pound) oven-ready chicken
1 cup hot chicken stock
1 (14½-ounce) can diced tomatoes
1 teaspoon ground cumin
salt and pepper, to taste

It couldn't be any easier to create a great-tasting meal. Just cook some rice or pasta, toss some salad greens in a bowl, and you're ready to serve.

1. Drain and rinse the beans and put into a saucepan, cover with cold water, and bring to a boil. Boil rapidly for 10 minutes, then remove from the heat and drain and rinse again.

2. Transfer the beans to the slow cooker and add the onion and chipotle pepper. Place the chicken on top, pour the stock and tomatoes with their can juices over it, sprinkle with cumin, and season with salt and pepper.

3. Cover and cook for 4 hours on high. Carefully remove the chicken and cut into eight parts. Skim the excess fat from the juices and adjust the seasoning.

4. Spoon the beans into a warm serving dish, top with the chicken, and spoon the juices over the top. Serve immediately.

CHICKEN BREASTS STUFFED WITH HERBED GOAT CHEESE

serves **4**

8 ounces soft, fresh goat cheese

¼ cup finely chopped fresh basil leaves

2 scallions, thinly sliced

2 garlic cloves, finely chopped

4 boneless, skinless chicken breasts

2 tablespoons olive oil

3 cups sliced Swiss chard
  (with the thick ribs removed)

1 cup dry white wine, chicken stock,
  or water

salt and pepper, to taste

Filling chicken breasts with herb-studded goat cheese turns them into sophisticated dinner party fare.

1. Put the cheese, basil, scallions, and garlic into a mixing bowl and stir to combine.

2. Lay the chicken breasts flat on a cutting board. Working with one breast at a time, place your hand on top of the breast and press down to keep it in place. With the other hand, using a large, sharp chef's knife, slice the breast horizontally, leaving one edge intact like a hinge.

3. Open the butterflied breasts and spoon equal amounts of the cheese mixture onto one half of each. Fold closed and secure with wooden toothpicks or kitchen string. Season the breasts with salt and pepper.

4. Heat the oil in a large skillet over medium–high heat until hot, then add the chicken. Cook on one side for 4 minutes, until brown, then turn and cook on the other side for an additional 4 minutes, until brown.

5. Put the Swiss chard and the wine into the slow cooker. Arrange the stuffed chicken breasts on top of the Swiss chard, cover, and cook on high for about 2 hours or on low for about 4 hours, until the chicken is cooked through. Serve hot.

TURKEY & RICE CASSEROLE

serves **4**

1 tablespoon olive oil
1 pound turkey breast, diced
1 onion, diced
2 carrots, diced
2 celery stalks, sliced
4 cups sliced closed-cup mushrooms
1 cup long-grain rice
2 cups hot chicken stock
salt and pepper, to taste

A great low-fat recipe if you're counting the calories, and turkey makes a change from chicken, too. Serve with soy or chili sauce to accompany.

1. Heat the oil in a heavy skillet, add the turkey, and cook over high heat for 3–4 minutes, until lightly browned.

2. Combine the onion, carrots, celery, mushrooms, and rice in the slow cooker. Arrange the turkey on top, season well with salt and pepper, and pour the stock over the ingredients. Cover and cook on high for 2 hours.

3. Stir lightly with a fork to mix, adjust the seasoning, if necessary, and serve immediately.

TURKEY BREAST WITH BACON, LEEKS & PRUNES

serves **6–8**

4 ounces bacon strips
2 leeks, trimmed, white and light-green
  parts, thinly sliced
1 (4-pound) skinless, boneless
  turkey breast
3 tablespoons all-purpose flour
1 tablespoon olive oil, if needed
12 pitted prunes, halved
  (quartered, if large)
1 teaspoon crumbled dried thyme
  or 1 tablespoon finely chopped
  fresh thyme
1 cup chicken stock
salt and pepper, to taste

When a whole turkey is too much, this elegant dish using just turkey breast is perfect.

1. Heat a skillet over medium–high heat, then add the bacon and cook until just crisp. Remove from the pan, drain on paper towels, then chop or crumble into small pieces.

2. Add the leeks to the skillet and cook in the bacon fat over medium–high heat, stirring frequently, for about 5 minutes, or until soft.

3. Season the turkey with salt and pepper and dredge with the flour. If needed, add the oil to the skillet, then add the turkey and cook on one side for 4–5 minutes, until brown. Turn and cook on the other side for an additional 4–5 minutes, until brown.

4. Put the turkey into the slow cooker with the leeks, bacon, prunes, and thyme. Add the stock, cover, and cook on high for about 5 hours or on low for about 9 hours.

5. Remove the turkey from the slow cooker and let rest for 5 minutes. Slice and serve with some of the sauce, including the prunes and pieces of bacon, spooned over the top.

SAUSAGE & BEAN CASSEROLE

serves **4**

2 tablespoons sunflower oil
2 onions, chopped
2 garlic cloves, finely chopped
4 ounces bacon, chopped
1 pound pork sausages
1 (15-ounce) can cranberry beans or
red kidney beans, or black-eyed peas,
drained and rinsed
2 tablespoons chopped fresh parsley
²/₃ cup hot beef stock

To serve
4 slices French bread
¹/₂ cup shredded Gruyère cheese

Here is slow cooking at its best. This is a variation on a regional French casserole known as a cassoulet. Use good-quality link sausages to get the best results.

1. Heat the oil in a heavy skillet. Add the onions and cook over low heat, stirring occasionally, for 5 minutes, until softened. Add the garlic, bacon, and sausages and cook, stirring and turning the sausages occasionally, for an additional 5 minutes.

2. Using a slotted spoon, transfer the mixture from the skillet to the slow cooker. Add the beans, parsley, and stock, then cover and cook on low for 6 hours.

3. Shortly before serving, preheat the broiler. Put the bread slices onto the broiler rack and lightly toast on one side under the preheated broiler. Turn the slices over, sprinkle with the shredded cheese, and place under the broiler until just melted.

4. Serve the casserole and the bread slices immediately.

PORK CHOPS STUFFED WITH APPLES

serves **4**

1 large Granny Smith, Pippin, or
  Gala apple, peeled and sliced
½ cup apple juice or water
4 boneless pork chops, about 1 inch thick
4 slices prosciutto
4 ounces Gorgonzola cheese or
  other blue cheese
salt and pepper, to taste
mashed potatoes, to serve

A great taste combination with sweet apples, salty ham, and pungent blue cheese to offset the natural richness of the pork.

1. Place half of the apple slices in the bottom of the slow cooker and add the apple juice.

2. Butterfly the pork chops by laying each chop flat on a cutting board and, pressing down on it with the flat of your hand to keep it in place. Cut through the center horizontally, leaving one side attached like a hinge. Loosely wrap in plastic wrap and gently pound with a meat mallet to a thickness of about ¾ inch.

3. Open the flattened and butterflied chops like books and place on the cutting board. Layer each chop with a slice of prosciutto, one-quarter of the cheese, and one-quarter of the remaining apple slices. Fold closed and secure with wooden toothpicks.

4. Season the stuffed chops all over with salt and pepper and put into the slow cooker on top of the apple slices. Cover and cook on high for about 4 hours or on low for about 7 hours, until the meat is cooked through. Serve hot with mashed potatoes.

HAM COOKED IN CIDER

serves **6**

1 (2¼-pound) boneless ham
1 onion, halved
4 cloves
6 black peppercorns
1 teaspoon juniper berries
1 celery stalk, chopped
1 carrot, sliced
4 cups medium hard cider or apple juice
fresh salad, to serve

A ham can make a great midweek roast, and cooking it this way will help to keep the meat moist. Any cold leftovers will make excellent sandwiches.

1. Place a trivet or rack in the slow cooker, if you like, and stand the ham on it. Otherwise, just put the ham into the slow cooker. Stud each onion half with two of the cloves and add to the slow cooker with the peppercorns, juniper berries, celery, and carrot.

2. Pour in the cider, cover, and cook on low for 8 hours, until the meat is tender.

3. Remove the ham from the cooker and put onto a board. Tent with aluminum foil and let stand for 10–15 minutes. Discard the cooking liquid and flavorings.

4. Cut off any rind and fat from the ham and carve into slices. Transfer to serving plates and serve immediately with a fresh salad.

BEEF SHORT RIBS BRAISED IN RED WINE

serves **6**

1 (3-pound) bone-in beef short ribs
2 tablespoons vegetable oil, plus extra,
  if needed
1 onion, diced
1 celery stalk, diced
1 carrot, diced
1 tablespoon tomato paste
3 fresh thyme sprigs
2 garlic cloves, finely chopped
3 tablespoons all-purpose flour
2 cups red wine
1 cup beef stock
1 bay leaf
salt and pepper, to taste
mashed potatoes or cooked polenta,
  to serve

If possible, ask your butcher to cut the ribs into thirds for easier serving.

1. Generously season the ribs with salt and pepper. Heat the oil in a large, heavy skillet over medium–high heat. Add the ribs and cook, turning occasionally, for about 10 minutes, until brown on all sides. Transfer to the slow cooker.

2. Add more oil to the skillet, if needed, and, when hot, add the onion, celery, and carrot. Cook, stirring occasionally, for about 15 minutes, until the vegetables are soft. Add the tomato paste, thyme, garlic, and flour and cook, stirring, for an additional 1 minute.

3. Add the wine, bring to a boil, and cook for an additional 1–2 minutes, stirring and scraping up any sediment from the bottom of the skillet. Reduce the heat to medium–low and simmer for 6–8 minutes, until the liquid is reduced by about half. Transfer to the slow cooker.

4. Stir in the stock, $\frac{1}{2}$ teaspoon of salt, and the bay leaf, cover, and cook on high for 7 hours or on low for 10 hours, until the meat is tender and falling from the bone. About 1–2 hours before the end of cooking, set the lid ajar, if desired, to let the liquid reduce and reach a thicker consistency.

5. Before serving, remove and discard the thyme and bay leaf. Serve hot with the mashed potatoes.

POT ROAST WITH BEER

serves **4–6**

2 small onions, each cut into
  8 wedges
8 small carrots, halved lengthwise
1 fennel bulb, cut into 8 wedges
1 (5-pound) rolled chuck steak
2 tablespoons Dijon mustard
1 tablespoon all-purpose flour
½ cup beer
salt and pepper, to taste

There are many great beers that you can try in this recipe, although the darker ones will produce the best flavor. Serve accompanied by buttery mashed potatoes.

1. Put the onions, carrots, and fennel into the slow cooker and season with salt and pepper. Place the beef on top.

2. Mix together the mustard and flour to form a paste and spread it over the beef. Season well and pour the beer over the top. Cover and cook on low for 8 hours.

3. Remove the beef and vegetables with a slotted spoon and transfer to a warm serving platter. Skim the excess fat from the juices and pour the juices into a gravy boat or small pitcher to serve with the beef. Serve immediately.

STEAK ROLL UPS WITH SPINACH & FETA CHEESE

serves **4**

4 chuck steaks (about 1½ pounds
  in total), pounded to a thickness
  of 1½ inch
½ onion, diced
¾ cup crumbled feta cheese
¼ cup chopped, pitted Kalamata olives
4 small handfuls baby spinach leaves
¼ cup beef stock or water
salt and pepper, to taste

*Rolling steak around a flavorsome filling
makes for an elegant presentation of a
surprisingly simple dish.*

1. Season the steaks on both sides with salt and pepper. Top each steak with one-quarter each of the onion, cheese, olives, and spinach. Starting with one of the short sides, roll up the steaks into pinwheels and secure with kitchen string or wooden toothpicks.

2. Place the steak rolls in the slow cooker along with the stock, cover, and cook on high for about 3 hours or on low for 6 hours, until the meat is tender and cooked through. Serve hot.

LAMB SHANKS WITH OLIVES

serves **4**

1½ tablespoons all-purpose flour
4 lamb shanks
2 tablespoons olive oil
1 onion, sliced
2 garlic cloves, finely chopped
2 teaspoons sweet paprika
1 (14-ounce) can diced tomatoes
2 tablespoons tomato paste
2 carrots, sliced
2 teaspoons sugar
1 cup red wine
1 (2-inch) cinnamon stick
2 fresh rosemary sprigs
1 cup pitted, ripe black olives
2 tablespoons lemon juice
2 tablespoons chopped fresh mint,
  plus extra leaves to garnish
salt and pepper, to taste

1. Put the flour into a plastic food bag and season with salt and pepper. Add the lamb shanks, hold the top securely, and shake well to coat.

2. Heat the oil in a large, heavy saucepan. Add the lamb shanks and cook over medium heat, turning frequently, for 6–8 minutes, until evenly browned. Transfer to a plate and set aside.

3. Add the onion and garlic to the saucepan and cook, stirring frequently, for 5 minutes, until softened. Stir in the paprika and cook for 1 minute. Add the tomatoes, tomato paste, carrots, sugar, wine, cinnamon stick, and rosemary and bring to a boil.

4. Transfer the mixture to the slow cooker and add the lamb shanks. Cover and cook on low for 8 hours, until the lamb is tender.

5. Add the olives, lemon juice, and chopped mint to the slow cooker. Replace the lid and cook on high for 30 minutes. Remove and discard the rosemary and cinnamon stick. Transfer to warm serving plates, garnish with mint leaves, and serve immediately.

HONEY-GLAZED DUCK LEGS

serves **4–6**

6 duck legs
½ cup chicken stock
3 tablespoons red wine or white wine
½ cup honey
1 tablespoon fresh thyme leaves
salt and pepper, to taste
mashed potatoes, to serve

This elegant alternative to chicken legs is a great dinner party dish.

1. Trim any excess skin or fat from the duck legs and season with salt and pepper. Heat a large, heavy skillet over medium–high heat. When the skillet is hot, add the duck legs, in batches if necessary, and cook on one side for about 4 minutes, until brown. Turn and cook on the other side for about 4 minutes, until brown. Transfer to the slow cooker.

2. Put the stock, wine, honey, and thyme into a small bowl, stir to combine, then pour the mixture over the duck legs, turning to coat. Cover and cook on high for about 6 hours or on low for about 10 hours, until the duck is tender. Serve hot with mashed potatoes.

SEAFOOD STEW

serves **4**

2 tablespoons olive oil, plus extra
 for drizzling
1 large onion, chopped
4 garlic cloves, finely chopped
1 yellow bell pepper, seeded and chopped
1 red bell pepper, seeded and chopped
1 orange bell pepper, seeded
 and chopped
4 tomatoes, peeled and chopped
2 large mild green chiles,
 such as poblano, chopped
finely grated rind and juice of 1 lime
2 tablespoons chopped fresh cilantro,
 plus extra leaves to garnish
1 bay leaf
2 cups fish, vegetable, or chicken stock
1 pound red snapper fillets
1 pound shrimp
8 ounces prepared squid
salt and pepper, to taste

The flavors of lime and fresh cilantro leaves give this healthy yet hearty fish stew a rich flavor.

1. Heat the oil in a saucepan. Add the onion and garlic and cook over low heat, stirring occasionally, for 5 minutes, until softened. Add the bell peppers, tomatoes, and chiles and cook, stirring frequently, for 5 minutes. Stir in the lime rind and juice, add the chopped cilantro and bay leaf, and pour in the stock. Bring to a boil, stirring occasionally.

2. Transfer the mixture to the slow cooker, cover, and cook on low for 7½ hours. Meanwhile, skin the fish fillets, if necessary, and cut the flesh into chunks. Peel and devein the shrimp. Cut the squid bodies into rings and halve the tentacles or leave them whole.

3. Add the seafood to the stew, season with salt and pepper, replace the lid, and cook on high for 30 minutes, or until tender and cooked through. Remove and discard the bay leaf. Transfer to warm serving bowls, garnish with cilantro leaves, and serve immediately.

EASY BOUILLABAISSE WITH GARLIC MAYONNAISE

serves **4**

pinch of saffron threads
1 tablespoon hot water
2 tablespoons olive oil
1 onion, diced
3 garlic cloves, finely chopped
2 celery stalks, finely chopped
2 teaspoons crumbled, dried oregano
1 teaspoon salt
$^{1}/_{4}$–$^{1}/_{2}$ teaspoon crushed dried red
  pepper flakes
$1^{1}/_{2}$ cups dry white wine
$1^{1}/_{2}$ cups canned tomato paste
1 (14-ounce) can diced tomatoes,
  with juice
12 small clams, scrubbed
12 mussels, scrubbed and debearded
1 pound white fish fillet, such as
  halibut, cut into 2-inch pieces
8 ounces shrimp, peeled and deveined
2 tablespoons finely chopped fresh
  parsley, to garnish

Garlic mayonnaise
2 garlic cloves, finely chopped
$^{1}/_{2}$ teaspoon salt
$^{1}/_{2}$ cup mayonnaise

This simplified version of the French classic is sure to impress. Feel free to add or substitute other types of fish or shellfish.

1. Put the saffron into a small bowl and cover with the hot water. Heat the oil in a large skillet over medium–high heat. Add the onion and garlic and cook, stirring, for about 5 minutes, until soft. Add the celery, oregano, salt, and red pepper flakes, then add the wine. Bring to a boil and cook, stirring, for about 8 minutes, until the liquid is reduced by half. Transfer the mixture to the slow cooker.

2. Stir in the saffron and its soaking water, tomato paste, and tomatoes with their can juices. Cover and cook on high for about 2 hours or on low for about 4 hours.

3. Discard any clams or mussels with broken shells and any that refuse to close when tapped. Add the fish, shrimp, clams, and mussels, cover, and cook on high for an additional 10–15 minutes, until the fish and shrimp are cooked through and the clams and mussels have opened, discarding any that still remain closed.

4. To make the garlic mayonnaise, mash together the garlic and salt, using a fork to make a paste. Stir in the mayonnaise. To serve, ladle some broth into four serving bowls, then add some of the fish and shellfish. Top each serving with a dollop of the garlic mayonnaise, garnish with parsley, and serve immediately.

SALMON WITH DILL & LIME

serves **4**

3 tablespoons butter, melted

1 onion, thinly sliced

4 red-skinned or white round potatoes, thinly sliced

½ cup hot fish stock or water

4 pieces skinless salmon fillet (about 5 ounces each)

juice of 1 lime

2 tablespoons chopped fresh dill

salt and pepper, to taste

lime wedges, to serve

The delicate flavor of salmon is retained in this simply cooked fish dish. Serve with tender green beans or peas for an elegant lunch or dinner.

1. Brush the bottom of the slow cooker with 1 tablespoon of the butter. Layer the onion and potatoes in the dish, sprinkling with salt and pepper between the layers. Add the stock and drizzle with 1 tablespoon of the butter. Cover and cook on low for 3 hours.

2. Arrange the salmon over the vegetables in a single layer. Drizzle the lime juice over the ingredients, sprinkle with the dill, season with salt and pepper, and pour the remaining butter on top. Cover and cook on low for an additional 1 hour, until the fish flakes easily.

3. Serve the salmon and vegetables on warm plates with the juices spooned over the top and lime wedges on the side.

CLAMS IN SPICY BROTH

serves **4**

1 tablespoon olive oil

1 red onion, halved lengthwise
  and sliced

4 ounces chorizo or other spicy
  sausage, diced

1 fennel bulb, coarsely chopped

1 (14-ounce) can diced tomatoes,
  with juice

½ cup dry white wine

½ cup clam juice or water

½ teaspoon salt

¼–½ teaspoon crushed red pepper flakes

2 pounds small clams, scrubbed

2 tablespoons chopped fresh
  flat-leaf parsley, to garnish

green salad and crusty bread, to serve

This festive, yet simple shellfish dish makes a lovely light meal served with a crisp green salad and plenty of fresh crusty bread for soaking up the delicious broth.

1. Heat the oil in a large skillet over medium–high heat. Add the onion and cook, stirring, for about 5 minutes, until soft. Add the chorizo and continue to cook, stirring occasionally, until the meat begins to brown. Transfer the mixture to the slow cooker.

2. Stir in the fennel, tomatoes and their can juices, wine, clam juice, salt, and red pepper flakes. Cover and cook on high for about 2 hours or on low for about 4 hours.

3. Discard any clams with broken shells and any that refuse to close when tapped. Add the clams to the slow cooker, cover, and cook on high for an additional 10–15 minutes, until the clams have opened. Discard any clams that remain closed.

4. Serve the clams in bowls, with a generous amount of broth, garnished with parsley, and accompanied by a green salad and crusty bread.

SEA BREAM IN LEMON SAUCE

serves **4**

8 sea bream fillets
4 tablespoons unsalted butter
3 tablespoons all-purpose flour
3½ cups warm milk
¼ cup lemon juice
4 cups sliced button mushrooms
1 bouquet garni (sprigs of parsley, bay
  leaf, and thyme tied together)
salt and pepper, to taste
lemon wedges and grilled asparagus,
  to serve

*Use red snapper or sea bass if sea bream
is not available for this simple yet
delicious fish dish with a lemon-flavored
mushroom sauce.*

1. Put the fish fillets into the slow cooker and set aside.

2. Melt the butter in a saucepan over low heat. Add the flour
and cook, stirring continuously, for 1 minute. Gradually stir
in the milk, a little at a time, and bring to a boil, stirring
continuously. Stir in the lemon juice and mushrooms, add the
bouquet garni, and season with salt and pepper. Reduce the
heat and simmer for 5 minutes. Pour the sauce over the fish
fillets, cover, and cook on low for 1½ hours.

3. Carefully lift out the fish fillets and transfer to warm serving
plates. Serve immediately with lemon wedges and asparagus.

HALIBUT WITH FENNEL & OLIVES

serves **4**

vegetable oil, for brushing

2 tablespoons olive oil

½ cup chopped, pitted Kalamata olives

1 garlic clove, finely chopped

1 small shallot, finely chopped

zest of 1 lemon

1 tablespoon finely chopped
  fresh oregano

1 fennel bulb, thinly sliced

4 halibut fillets (about 6 ounces each)

¼ cup dry white wine

cooked couscous, to serve

Fresh fennel adds a unique flavor to this simple halibut dish.

1. Lightly brush four 12-inch square pieces of parchment paper with vegetable oil.

2. Put the olive oil, olives, garlic, shallot, lemon zest, and oregano into a bowl and mix to combine.

3. Pile equal amounts of the fennel slices in the middle of the prepared pieces of parchment paper. Top each pile of fennel with a halibut fillet. Spoon the olive mixture over the fish.

4. Drizzle the wine over the fish. Fold up the packages, leaving a little room for steam circulation, and place them in the slow cooker. Cover and cook on high for about 2 hours, until the fish is cooked through.

5. To serve, open up the packages and gently transfer the contents to warm plates. Serve immediately with couscous.

CHAPTER 4
VEGETARIAN

Baked Eggs with Melted Onions 140

Winter Vegetable Medley 142

Vegetable Pasta 145

Louisiana Zucchini 146

Butternut Squash & Goat Cheese Enchiladas 148

Summer Vegetable Casserole 151

Wild Mushroom Lasagna 152

Vegetable Stew with Parsley Dumpling 155

Pumpkin Risotto 156

Vegetable Curry 159

Spiced Chickpeas 160

Baked Eggplant with Zucchini 163

Tofu with Spicy Peanut Sauce 164

Mixed Bean Chili 167

Stuffed Butternut Squash 168

Macaroni & Cheese with Toasted Bread Crumbs 170

White Bean Stew 172

Vegetarian Paella 175

Spaghetti with Lentil Sauce 176

Asparagus & Spinach Risotto 179

BAKED EGGS WITH MELTED ONIONS

serves 4

4 tablespoons butter, plus extra
 for greasing
1 onion, halved and thinly sliced
¼ cup heavy cream
⅔ cup freshly grated vegetarian
 Parmesan-style cheese
4 extra-large eggs
8 small fresh sage leaves
salt and pepper, to taste

Perfectly cooked eggs served in a rich, creamy sauce make a beautiful brunch dish or a sophisticated first course.

1. Grease four ¾-cup ramekins with butter. Fill the slow cooker with hot water to a depth of 1 inch, cover, and turn on to high.

2. Melt the butter in a large skillet over medium–high heat. Add the onions and cook, stirring occasionally, for about 6 minutes, until soft and just beginning to brown. Reduce the heat to medium, add 3 tablespoons of the cream, and continue to cook, stirring occasionally, for an additional 5 minutes, or until the cream is beginning to thicken.

3. Stir in the cheese. Season the mixture with salt and pepper and divide among the prepared ramekins.

4. Break an egg into each ramekin, season with a little more salt and pepper, then top each egg with two sage leaves and evenly drizzle the remaining cream over the eggs.

5. Cover each ramekin with aluminum foil and place carefully in the water bath in the slow cooker. Cover the slow cooker and cook on high for about 1 hour, until the eggs are set to your liking. Serve hot in the ramekins.

WINTER VEGETABLE MEDLEY

serves **4**

2 tablespoons sunflower oil
2 onions, chopped
3 carrots, chopped
3 parsnips, chopped
2 bunches celery, chopped
2 tablespoons chopped fresh parsley
1 tablespoon chopped fresh cilantro
1¼ cups vegetable stock
salt and pepper, to taste

Serve this herb-flavored vegetable stew with brown rice or pasta for a tasty and nutritious meal. Toasted seeds or nuts sprinkled on top will give crunch.

1. Heat the oil in a large, heavy saucepan. Add the onions and cook over medium heat, stirring occasionally, for 5 minutes, until softened. Add the carrots, parsnips, and celery and cook, stirring occasionally, for an additional 5 minutes. Stir in the herbs, season with salt and pepper, and pour in the stock. Bring to a boil.

2. Transfer the vegetable mixture to the slow cooker, cover, and cook on high for 3 hours, until tender. Taste and adjust the seasoning, if necessary. Using a slotted spoon, transfer the medley to warm plates, then spoon a little of the cooking liquid over the top. Serve immediately.

VEGETABLE PASTA

serves **4**

8 ounces dried penne pasta
2 tablespoons olive oil, plus extra
  for drizzling
1 red onion, sliced
2 zucchini, thinly sliced
3 cups sliced closed-cup mushrooms
2 tablespoons chopped fresh oregano
3 tomatoes, sliced
⅔ cup freshly grated vegetarian
  Parmesan-style cheese
salt and pepper, to taste

Layers of pasta and sliced vegetables with a sprinkling of fresh herbs and vegetarian cheese will make a satisfying meal for any occasion.

1. Bring a large saucepan of lightly salted water to a boil. Add the pasta, bring back to a boil, and cook according to the package directions until tender but still firm to the bite. Drain. Meanwhile, heat the oil in a heavy saucepan, add the onion, and cook over medium heat, stirring occasionally, for 5 minutes, until softened. Stir into the pasta.

2. Arrange a layer of zucchini and mushrooms in the slow cooker and top with a layer of pasta. Sprinkle with oregano, season with salt and peppe,r and continue layering, finishing with a layer of vegetables.

3. Arrange the sliced tomatoes on top and drizzle with oil. Cover and cook on high for 3 hours, or until tender.

4. Sprinkle with cheese, cover, and cook for an additional 10 minutes. Transfer to a warm bowl and serve immediately.

LOUISIANA ZUCCHINI

serves **6**

7 zucchini (about 2¼ pounds),
  thickly sliced
1 onion, finely chopped
2 garlic cloves, finely chopped
2 red bell peppers, seeded and chopped
⅓ cup hot vegetable stock
4 tomatoes, peeled and chopped
2 tablespoons butter, diced
salt and cayenne pepper, to taste
crusty bread, to serve

Use a mixture of green zucchini and yellow squash for added color in this simple vegetable recipe. You can serve it as a side dish to nonvegetarians.

1. Put the zucchini, onion, garlic, and red bell peppers into the slow cooker and season with salt and cayenne pepper. Pour in the stock and mix well.

2. Sprinkle the chopped tomatoes on top and dot with the butter. Cover and cook on high for 2½ hours, until tender. Serve immediately with crusty bread.

BUTTERNUT SQUASH & GOAT CHEESE ENCHILADAS

serves **4**

1 large butternut squash,
 peeled and diced
¼ cup olive oil
1 teaspoon salt
1 tablespoon ground cumin
1 large onion, diced
3 garlic cloves, finely chopped
1 tablespoon hot or mild chili powder
1 tablespoon dried oregano
1¾ cups tomato puree or tomato sauce
1 tablespoon honey
2 cups vegetable stock
12 corn tortillas
8 ounces soft, fresh goat cheese

Roasting butternut squash caramelizes it, giving an enticing sweetness that balances out the spicy sauce and salty cheese.

1. Preheat the oven to 400°F. Line a baking sheet with parchment paper. Coat the squash with 2 tablespoons of the oil, then sprinkle with half the salt and 1 teaspoon of the cumin. Put the squash onto the prepared sheet and roast for 30–40 minutes, until soft and beginning to brown.

2. Heat the remaining oil in a large skillet over medium–high heat. Add the onion and garlic and cook, stirring, for about 5 minutes, until soft. Add the remaining cumin and salt, the chili powder, and oregano and cook for an additional 1 minute. Stir in the tomato puree, honey, and stock, bring to a boil, and cook for about 5 minutes. Puree the sauce in a food processor or blender.

3. Coat the bottom of the slow cooker with a little sauce. Make a layer of tortillas, tearing them, if necessary, to cover the bottom of the slow cooker. Top the tortillas with a layer of the squash, a layer of cheese, a layer of sauce, then another layer of tortillas.

4. Layer again with squash, cheese, and sauce. Finish with a layer of tortillas, sauce, and the remaining cheese. Cover and cook on low for 2 hours, until the tortillas are soft and the cheese is melted and bubbling. Serve hot.

SUMMER VEGETABLE CASSEROLE

serves **4**

4 Yukon gold or white round potatoes,
  cubed

2 zucchini, cubed

2 red bell peppers, seeded and cubed

2 red onions, sliced

2 teaspoons mixed dried herbs

1 cup hot vegetable stock

salt and pepper, to taste

As an alternative, use sliced new potatoes with the skin left on for extra nutritional value. You can add other summer vegetables that are available to vary the recipe.

1. Layer all the vegetables in the slow cooker, sprinkling with herbs and salt and pepper between the layers.

2. Pour the stock over the vegetables. Cover and cook on low for 7 hours. Transfer to warm serving bowls and serve immediately.

WILD MUSHROOM LASAGNA

serves **4–6**

vegetable oil, for brushing
12 lasagna noodles
¼ cup freshly grated vegetarian
  Parmesan-style cheese

Filling
1 ounce dried porcini
2 cups boiling water
2 tablespoons olive oil
1 small onion, diced
2 garlic cloves, finely chopped
6½ cups sliced button mushrooms
  or chestnut mushrooms
½ cup red wine
1 tablespoon finely chopped fresh
  thyme leaves
½ teaspoon salt
½ teaspoon pepper

Sauce
4 tablespoons unsalted butter
¼ cup all-purpose flour
2½ cups milk
1 cup freshly grated vegetarian
  Parmesan-style cheese
¾ teaspoon salt

1. To make the filling, soak the porcini in the water for 30 minutes. Remove the mushrooms, reserving the liquid, and chop. Heat the oil in a large skillet over medium–high heat. Add the onion and garlic and cook, stirring, for 5 minutes. Add the fresh and reconstituted mushrooms and cook, stirring, for about 5 minutes, until soft. Add the wine, bring to a boil, and cook for about 5 minutes, until the liquid has almost evaporated. Add the mushroom soaking liquid, thyme, salt, and pepper and cook over medium–high heat, stirring frequently, for an additional 5 minutes, or until the liquid is reduced by half.

2. To make the sauce, melt the butter in a large saucepan over medium heat. Whisk in the flour and cook, whisking continuously, for about 3 minutes, until the mixture is golden brown. Whisk in the milk and bring to a boil. Reduce the heat and simmer for 3 minutes, then remove from the heat and stir in the cheese and salt.

3. To assemble the lasagna, line the slow cooker with aluminum foil, overlapping two large pieces to cover the entire bottom. Lightly brush the foil with oil. Spoon a thin layer of sauce and a thin layer of mushrooms over the bottom. Top with a layer of pasta. Repeat, to make a total of three layers. Top with a final layer of pasta, then a layer of sauce. Sprinkle the cheese over the top. Cover and cook on low for about 4 hours, until the pasta is tender and the top is brown and bubbling. Serve the lasagna directly from the slow cooker, or use the foil as a sling to lift it out to serve.

VEGETABLE STEW WITH PARSLEY DUMPLINGS

serves **6**

½ large sweet potato, cut into chunks
2 onions, sliced
2 Yukon gold or white round potatoes,
  cut into chunks
2 carrots, cut into chunks
2 celery stalks, sliced
2 zucchini, sliced
2 tablespoons tomato paste
2½ cups hot vegetable stock
1 bay leaf
1 teaspoon ground coriander
½ teaspoon dried thyme
2½ cups drained, canned corn kernels
salt and pepper, to taste

Parsley dumplings
1¾ cups all-purpose flour
1¾ teaspoons baking powder
pinch of salt
½ cup vegetable shortening
2 tablespoons chopped fresh
  flat-leaf parsley, plus extra sprigs
  to garnish
about ½ cup milk

Nonvegetarians won't miss the meat in this vegetable stew if they have light and fluffy herb dumplings on their plates.

1. Put the sweet potato, onions, potatoes, carrots, celery, and zucchini into the slow cooker. Stir the tomato paste into the stock and pour the liquid over the vegetables. Add the bay leaf, coriander, and thyme and season with salt and pepper. Cover and cook on low for 6 hours.

2. To make the dumplings, sift the flour with the baking powder and salt into a bowl and stir in the shortening and chopped parsley. Add just enough of the milk to make a firm but light dough. Knead lightly and shape into 12 small balls.

3. Stir the corn kernels into the vegetable mixture in the slow cooker and place the dumplings on top. Cook on high for 30 minutes. Transfer to warm serving plates, garnish with parsley sprigs, and serve immediately.

PUMPKIN RISOTTO

serves **4**

2 tablespoons olive oil
1 shallot, finely chopped
1 garlic clove, finely chopped
1½ cups risotto rice
½ cup dry white wine
5 cups vegetable stock
1 (15-ounce) can pumpkin puree
1 tablespoon finely chopped fresh sage
½ teaspoon salt
¼ teaspoon pepper
pinch of nutmeg
2 tablespoons butter
1⅓ cups freshly grated vegetarian
   Parmesan-style cheese, plus extra
   to serve

This stunning risotto, enriched with delicious pumpkin puree, is a satisfying vegetarian main dish for a festive meal any time of the year.

1. Heat the oil in a large skillet over medium–high heat. Add the shallot and garlic and cook, stirring, for about 5 minutes, until soft. Add the rice and cook, stirring, for 1 minute. Add the wine and cook for an additional 3 minutes, until the liquid is absorbed. Transfer the mixture to the slow cooker.

2. Stir in the stock, pumpkin puree, sage, salt, pepper, and nutmeg. Cover and cook on high for about 1½ hours, until the rice is tender. Stir in the butter, replace the lid, and cook for an additional 15 minutes. Stir in the cheese and serve immediately, with a little more cheese sprinkled over the top.

VEGETABLE CURRY

serves **4–6**

2 tablespoons vegetable oil
1 teaspoon cumin seeds
1 onion, sliced
2 curry leaves
1-inch piece fresh ginger,
  finely chopped
2 fresh red chiles, seeded
  and chopped
2 tablespoons Indian curry paste
2 carrots, sliced
1 cup snow peas
1 cauliflower, cut into florets
3 tomatoes, peeled and chopped
½ cup frozen peas, thawed
½ teaspoon ground turmeric
⅔–1 cup hot vegetable stock
salt and pepper, to taste
naan bread, to serve

Every cook should have a great vegetable curry recipe, and this could be the one. For nonvegetarians, it could also be served as an accompaniment to a meat or chicken curry.

1. Heat the oil in a large, heavy saucepan. Add the cumin seeds and cook, stirring continuously, for 1–2 minutes, until they release their aroma and begin to pop. Add the onion and curry leaves and cook, stirring occasionally, for 5 minutes, until the onion has softened. Add the ginger and chiles and cook, stirring occasionally, for 1 minute.

2. Stir in the curry paste and cook, stirring, for 2 minutes, then add the carrots, snow peas, and cauliflower. Cook for 5 minutes, then add the tomatoes, peas, and turmeric and season with salt and pepper. Cook for 3 minutes, then add ⅔ cup of the stock and bring to a boil.

3. Transfer the mixture to the slow cooker. If the vegetables are not covered by the liquid, add more hot stock, then cover and cook on low for 5 hours, until tender. Remove and discard the curry leaves. Transfer to warm serving dishes and serve immediately with naan bread.

SPICED CHICKPEAS

serves **4**

2 tablespoons vegetable oil
1 onion, finely chopped
2 garlic cloves, finely chopped
1 teaspoon ground cumin
1 teaspoon ground turmeric
1 teaspoon ground ginger
¼–½ teaspoon cayenne pepper
1½ cups water
2 (15-ounce) cans chickpeas,
  rinsed and drained
1 teaspoon salt
½ teaspoon garam masala

To serve
steamed rice
yogurt and cucumber salad

For a healthy and delicious meal, serve these spicy chickpeas with steamed rice and a cooling yogurt and cucumber salad.

1. Heat the oil in a large skillet over medium–high heat. Add the onion and garlic and cook, stirring, for about 5 minutes, until soft. Add the cumin, turmeric, ginger, and cayenne pepper and cook, stirring, for an additional 1 minute. Add the water and cook for an additional 1–2 minutes, scraping up any sediment from the bottom of the skillet. Transfer the mixture to the slow cooker.

2. Stir in the chickpeas, cover, and cook on low for about 6 hours.

3. Just before serving, add the salt and garam masala. Serve hot with rice, along with a yogurt and cucumber salad.

BAKED EGGPLANT WITH ZUCCHINI

serves **4**

2 large eggplants
olive oil, for brushing
2 large zucchini, sliced
4 tomatoes, sliced
1 garlic clove, finely chopped
3 tablespoons dry bread crumbs
3 tablespoons freshly grated
  vegetarian Parmesan-style cheese
salt and pepper, to taste
basil leaves, to garnish

Here is a Mediterranean-inspired dish that combines the vegetable mixture of ratatouille in a crumb-topped casserole. Fresh basil just adds the final flavor.

1. Cut the eggplants into fairly thin slices and brush with oil. Heat a large, ridged grill pan or heavy skillet over high heat, then add the eggplants and cook in batches for 6–8 minutes, turning once, until soft and brown.

2. Layer the eggplants in the slow cooker with the zucchini, tomatoes, and garlic, seasoning with salt and pepper between the layers.

3. Mix the bread crumbs with the cheese and sprinkle the mixture over the vegetables. Cover and cook on low for 4 hours.

4. Transfer to warm serving bowls, garnish with basil leaves, and serve immediately.

TOFU WITH SPICY PEANUT SAUCE

serves **4**

1¹/₂ pounds extra-firm tofu
2 tablespoons vegetable oil
¹/₃ cup smooth peanut butter
3 tablespoons low-sodium soy sauce
3 tablespoons unseasoned rice vinegar
juice of 1 lime
2 tablespoons packed light brown sugar
2 teaspoons toasted sesame oil
2 garlic cloves, finely chopped
1 tablespoon finely chopped fresh ginger
2 jalapeño chiles, cored,
  seeded, and finely chopped
1 (12-ounce) package baby
  spinach leaves
chopped fresh cilantro, to serve
steamed rice, to serve

Nutritious tofu gets a powerful punch of flavor from a combination of peanut butter, garlic, chilies, and cilantro.

1. Slice the tofu into 1-inch-thick slabs and pat dry with paper towels, pressing to release any excess moisture. Cut into 1-inch cubes.

2. Heat the vegetable oil in a large, nonstick skillet over medium–high heat. Add the tofu, in batches, if necessary, and cook on one side for about 3 minutes, until brown. Turn and cook on the other side for an additional 3 minutes, until brown.

3. Meanwhile, put the peanut butter, soy sauce, vinegar, lime juice, sugar, sesame oil, garlic, ginger, and chiles into the slow cooker and mix to combine.

4. Add the tofu to the slow cooker. Stir gently to coat, cover, and cook on low for about 4 hours.

5. About 15 minutes before serving, place the spinach in the slow cooker on top of the cooked tofu mixture, cover, and cook for about 15 minutes, until the spinach is wilted. Stir in the cilantro and serve immediately with steamed rice.

MIXED BEAN CHILI

serves **4–6**

⅔ cup dried red kidney beans,
  soaked overnight, drained, and rinsed
⅔ cup dried black beans, soaked
  overnight, drained, and rinsed
⅔ cup dried pinto beans, soaked
  overnight, drained, and rinsed
2 tablespoons vegetable oil
1 onion, chopped
1 garlic clove, finely chopped
1 fresh red chile, seeded and chopped
1 yellow bell pepper, seeded and chopped
1 teaspoon ground cumin
1 tablespoon chili powder
4 cups vegetable stock
1 tablespoon sugar
salt and pepper, to taste
chopped fresh cilantro, to garnish
crusty bread, to serve

Serve a warming bowl of this comfort food with baked potato wedges and an avocado, tomato, and onion salad. If you eat dairy products, top with sour cream.

1. Put all the beans into a saucepan, cover with fresh cold water, and bring to a boil. Boil rapidly for at least 10 minutes, then remove from the heat, drain, and rinse again.

2. Heat the oil in a large, heavy saucepan. Add the onion, garlic, chile, and yellow bell pepper and cook over medium heat, stirring occasionally, for 5 minutes. Stir in the cumin and chili powder and cook, stirring, for 1–2 minutes. Add the drained beans and stock and bring to a boil. Boil vigorously for 15 minutes.

3. Transfer the mixture to the slow cooker, cover, and cook on low for 10 hours, until the beans are tender.

4. Season with salt and pepper, then ladle about one-third into a bowl. Mash well with a potato masher, then return the mashed beans to the slow cooker and stir in the sugar. Transfer to warm serving bowls and garnish with chopped cilantro. Serve immediately with crusty bread.

STUFFED BUTTERNUT SQUASH

serves **4**

2 tablespoons olive oil

1 shallot, diced

2 garlic cloves, finely chopped

4 cups sliced Swiss chard
  (with ribs removed)

¾ teaspoon salt

1 teaspoon paprika

2 cups vegetable stock

1 cup quinoa

1 (15-ounce) can cannellini beans,
  rinsed and drained

¼ cup diced, pitted Kalamata olives

¾ cup crumbled feta cheese

2 tablespoons finely chopped fresh
  mint leaves

2 butternut squashes, halved and seeded

To make the squash easier to cut, make a slit in the skin and heat in the microwave on high for 3–5 minutes.

1. Heat the oil in a large skillet over medium–high heat. Add the shallot and garlic and cook, stirring, for about 5 minutes, until soft. Add the Swiss chard and cook for about 3 minutes, until wilted. Add the salt and paprika and cook for an additional 1 minute. Add the stock and quinoa and bring to a boil. Reduce the heat to low, cover, and simmer for 15–20 minutes, until the quinoa is cooked through.

2. Stir in the beans, olives, half of the cheese, and the mint.

3. Fill the slow cooker with water to a depth of ¼ inch. Divide the quinoa mixture among the squash halves, then place them in the slow cooker, stuffed-side up. Cover and cook on low for 6 hours.

4. Preheat the broiler. Remove the squash halves from the slow cooker and top with the remaining cheese. Cook under the preheated broiler for about 3 minutes, until the cheese is beginning to brown. Serve hot.

MACARONI & CHEESE WITH TOASTED BREAD CRUMBS

serves **4**

vegetable oil, for brushing

2 tablespoons butter

2 tablespoons all-purpose flour

$^2/_3$ cup vegetable stock

2 cups evaporated milk

$1^1/_2$ teaspoons dry mustard

$^1/_8$–$^1/_4$ teaspoon cayenne pepper

1 teaspoon salt

$1^2/_3$ cups shredded vegetarian Gruyère cheese

$1^1/_3$ cups shredded vegetarian fontina cheese

$^2/_3$ cup freshly grated vegetarian Parmesan-style cheese

12 ounces dried elbow macaroni

$1^1/_2$ cups water

Topping

2 thick slices French bread or sourdough bread

2 tablespoons butter

This classic comfort food is a breeze to make in the slow cooker. A toasted bread-crumb topping cooked on the stove adds a welcome crunch.

1. Line the slow cooker with aluminum foil and brush with some oil.

2. Melt the butter in a large skillet or saucepan over medium–high heat. Whisk in the flour and cook for 1 minute. Reduce the heat to medium and slowly add the stock, evaporated milk, mustard, cayenne pepper, and salt. Cook, stirring, for about 3–5 minutes, until thick. Add all the cheeses and whisk until melted. Add the macaroni and stir to mix well. Transfer to the slow cooker.

3. Add the water and stir to mix. Cover and cook on high for about 2 hours or on low for about 4 hours, until the macaroni is tender.

4. To make the topping, process the bread in a food processor to make crumbs. Melt the butter in a large skillet over medium heat until bubbling. Add the bread crumbs and cook, stirring frequently, for about 5 minutes, until toasted and golden brown.

5. Serve hot, topped with the bread crumbs.

WHITE BEAN STEW

serves **4**

2 tablespoons olive oil

1 onion, diced

2 garlic cloves, finely chopped

2 carrots, diced

2 celery stalks, diced

²/₃ cup tomato paste

1 teaspoon salt

¹/₂ teaspoon pepper

¹/₄–¹/₂ teaspoon crushed dried
   red pepper flakes

1 bay leaf

1 cup dry white wine

2 (15-ounce) cans cannellini beans,
   rinsed and drained

4 cups sliced Swiss chard or kale
   (with thick ribs removed)

1 cup water

¹/₄ cup freshly grated vegetarian
   Parmesan-style cheese, to serve

A satisfying dish on its own, this rich and healthy stew is even better topped with a poached egg.

1. Heat the oil in a large skillet over medium–high heat. Add the onion and garlic and cook, stirring, for about 5 minutes, until soft. Add the carrots and celery and cook for an additional few minutes. Stir in the tomato paste, salt, pepper, red pepper flakes, and bay leaf, then add the wine.

2. Bring to a boil and cook, stirring and scraping up any sediment from the bottom of the skillet, for about 5 minutes, until most of the liquid has evaporated. Transfer the mixture to the slow cooker.

3. Stir in the beans, Swiss chard, and water. Cover and cook on high for 3 hours or on low for 6 hours. Serve hot, garnished with the cheese.

VEGETARIAN PAELLA

serves **6**

¼ cup olive oil

1 Bermuda onion, sliced

2 garlic cloves, finely chopped

4 cups hot vegetable stock

large pinch of saffron threads,
  lightly crushed

1 yellow bell pepper, seeded and sliced

1 red bell pepper, seeded and sliced

1 large eggplant, diced

1¼ cups risotto rice

4 tomatoes, peeled and chopped

1⅔ cups sliced cremini mushrooms

1 cup halved green beans

1 (15-ounce) can cranberry beans,
  drained and rinsed

salt and pepper, to taste

A delicious vegetarian version of the Spanish classic. If you include fish and seafood in your diet, you could add cooked shrimp just before serving.

1. Heat the oil in a large skillet. Add the onion and garlic and cook over low heat, stirring occasionally, for 5 minutes, until softened. Put 3 tablespoons of the hot stock into a small bowl and stir in the saffron, then set aside to steep.

2. Add the bell peppers and eggplant to the skillet and cook, stirring occasionally, for 5 minutes. Add the rice and cook, stirring continuously, for 1 minute, until the grains are coated with oil and glistening. Pour in the remaining stock and add the tomatoes, mushrooms, green beans, and cranberry beans. Stir in the saffron mixture and season with salt and pepper.

3. Transfer the mixture to the slow cooker, cover, and cook on low for 2½–3 hours, until the rice is tender and the stock has been absorbed. Transfer to warm serving plates and serve immediately.

SPAGHETTI WITH LENTIL SAUCE

serves **4–6**

2 tablespoons olive oil
1 onion, diced
2 garlic cloves, finely chopped
1 carrot, diced
2 celery stalks, diced
4 large mushrooms, diced
1 tablespoon tomato paste
1 teaspoon salt
1 teaspoon crumbled dried oregano
1 bay leaf
1 (14-ounce) can diced tomatoes,
  with juice
¼ cup dried lentils
1 cup water
1 pound dried spaghetti

Here, good old spaghetti gets a healthy vegetarian makeover — and it doesn't skimp on flavor.

1. Heat the oil in a large skillet over medium–high heat. Add the onion and garlic and cook, stirring, for about 5 minutes, until soft. Add the carrot, celery, and mushrooms and continue to cook, stirring occasionally, for an additional 5 minutes, or until the mushrooms are soft. Stir in the tomato paste, salt, oregano, and bay leaf and cook, stirring, for an additional 1 minute. Transfer the mixture to the slow cooker.

2. Stir in the tomatoes with their can juices, lentils, and water. Cover and cook on high for 8 hours.

3. Just before serving, cook the spaghetti according to the package directions. Serve the hot sauce spooned over the spaghetti.

ASPARAGUS & SPINACH RISOTTO

serves **4**

2 tablespoons olive oil
4 shallots, finely chopped
1½ cups risotto rice
1 garlic clove, crushed
½ cup dry white wine
3½ cups vegetable stock
8 ounces asparagus spears
1 (6-ounce) package baby spinach leaves
½ cup freshly grated vegetarian
  Parmesan-style cheese
salt and pepper, to taste

Cooking risotto this way removes the tedious stirring usually associated with the Italian dish. Risotto rice is a type of short-grain rice that creates the right creaminess.

1. Heat the oil in a skillet, add the shallots, and sauté over medium heat, stirring, for 2–3 minutes. Add the rice and garlic and cook for an additional 2 minutes, stirring. Add the wine and let it boil for 30 seconds.

2. Transfer the rice mixture to the slow cooker, add the stock, and season with salt and pepper. Cover and cook on high for 2 hours, or until most of the liquid is absorbed.

3. Cut the asparagus into 1½-inch lengths. Stir it into the rice, then spread the spinach over the top. Replace the lid and cook on high for an additional 30 minutes, until the asparagus is just tender and the spinach is wilted.

4. Stir in the spinach with the cheese, then adjust the seasoning, if necessary, and serve immediately in warm bowls.

CHAPTER 5
DESSERTS & CAKES

CRÈME BRÛLÉE

serves **6**

1 vanilla bean
4 cups heavy cream
6 egg yolks
½ cup granulated sugar
⅓ cup firmly packed light brown sugar

Using this method to cook the custard gently will mean your crème brûlée won't curdle.

1. Using a sharp knife, split the vanilla bean in half lengthwise, scrape the seeds into a saucepan, and add the bean. Pour in the cream and bring just to a boil, stirring continuously. Remove from the heat, cover, and let steep for 20 minutes.

2. Whisk together the egg yolks and granulated sugar in a bowl until thoroughly mixed. Remove and discard the vanilla bean from the pan, then whisk the cream into the egg-yolk mixture. Strain the mixture into a bowl.

3. Divide the mixture among six ramekins and cover with aluminum foil. Stand the ramekins on a trivet in the slow cooker and pour in enough boiling water to come about halfway up the sides of the ramekins. Cover and cook on low for 3–3½ hours, until just set. Remove the slow cooker insert from the base and let cool completely, then remove the ramekins and chill in the refrigerator for at least 4 hours.

4. Preheat the broiler to high. Sprinkle the brown sugar evenly over the surface of each dessert, then cook under the preheated broiler for 30–60 seconds, until the sugar has melted and caramelized. Alternatively, you can use a chef's blowtorch. Return the ramekins to the refrigerator and chill for an additional hour before serving.

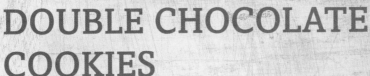

DOUBLE CHOCOLATE COOKIES

makes about **18**

1 cup all-purpose flour
1 cup unsweetened cocoa powder
½ teaspoon baking powder
¼ teaspoon salt
1 stick unsalted butter, softened,
  plus extra for greasing
½ cup granulated sugar
1 extra-large egg
1 teaspoon vanilla extract
2 tablespoons semisweet chocolate chips

Although they look more like brownies than traditional round cookies, these luxurious treats will win plenty of fans. The larger your slow cooker, the thinner these cookies will be. For best results, use a 1–1½-quart, round or oval slow cooker.

1. Generously grease the inside of the slow cooker with butter.

2. Put the flour, cocoa powder, baking powder, and salt into a medium bowl and mix to combine. Put the butter and sugar into a large bowl and cream together. Add the egg and vanilla extract and beat well together. Gradually beat in the flour mixture until well incorporated. Stir in the chocolate chips.

3. Using a rubber spatula, scrape the batter into the prepared slow cooker and smooth the top. Cover and cook on low for 2½ hours. Set the lid slightly ajar and continue to cook on low for an additional 30 minutes.

4. Keeping the cookie in the ceramic insert, remove it from the slow cooker and transfer to a wire rack to cool for 30 minutes. Turn out the cookie onto the rack and let cool for an additional 30 minutes before slicing it into 2-inch pieces. Serve at room temperature.

LEMON CAKE

serves **4**

¾ cup granulated sugar
3 eggs, separated
1¼ cups milk
3 tablespoons all-purpose flour, sifted
¼ teaspoon baking powder
⅔ cup lemon juice
confectioners' sugar, for dusting

This recipe will amaze you as the cooked batter separates to create a light cake sitting on top of a delicious lemony sauce.

1. Using an electric mixer, beat the granulated sugar with the egg yolks in a bowl. Gradually beat in the milk, followed by the flour and baking powder, and then the lemon juice.

2. Whisk the egg whites in a separate grease-free bowl until stiff. Fold half the whites into the yolk mixture, using a plastic spatula in a figure-eight movement, then fold in the remainder. Try not to knock out the air.

3. Pour the batter into a heatproof dish and cover with aluminum foil. Stand the dish on a trivet in the slow cooker and pour in enough boiling water to come about one-third of the way up the side of the dish. Cover and cook on high for 2½ hours, until the batter has set and the sauce and cake have separated.

4. Carefully remove the dish from the slow cooker and discard the foil. Transfer to warm bowls, lightly dust with confectioners' sugar, and serve immediately.

BROWN SUGAR APPLE CAKE

serves **6–8**

1½ cups all-purpose flour
½ teaspoon ground cinnamon
1¼ teaspoons baking powder
½ teaspoon baking soda
¼ teaspoon salt
1 stick unsalted butter, softened,
  plus extra for greasing
1 cup firmly packed light brown sugar
½ cup granulated sugar
2 extra-large eggs, lightly beaten
1 teaspoon vanilla extract
1 large apple, peeled, cored, and diced
whipped cream, to serve (optional)

This moist cinnamon-spiced apple cake is delicious for dessert, or as a sweet brunch treat. This recipe works best with a 3¾-quart slow cooker.

1. Grease the inside of the slow cooker with butter.

2. Put the flour, cinnamon, baking powder, baking soda, and salt into a medium bowl and mix to combine. Put the butter, brown sugar, and granulated sugar into a large bowl and cream together with an electric mixer.

3. Add the eggs and vanilla extract and beat on high for about 3 minutes. Gradually add the flour mixture to the sugar mixture, beating until fully incorporated. Stir in the apple.

4. Pour the mixture into the prepared slow cooker. Cover and cook on low for 2½–3 hours, until a toothpick inserted into the center of the cake comes out clean.

5. Keeping the cake in the ceramic insert, remove it from the slow cooker and transfer to a wire rack to cool for at least 60 minutes. Run a thin knife around the outside of the cake to release it from the sides of the insert, then turn it out onto a serving platter.

6. To serve, slice into wedges and top with a dollop of whipped cream, if using.

STRAWBERRY CHEESECAKE

serves **6–8**

6 tablespoons unsalted butter, melted

1¼ cups crushed graham crackers

1 pint strawberries, hulled

2½ cups cream cheese

1 cup granulated sugar

2 extra-large eggs, beaten

2 tablespoons cornstarch

finely grated rind and juice of 1 lemon

An excellent cheesecake with a creamy filling full of strawberry flavor. You could use raspberries instead, if you prefer.

1. Stir the butter into the crushed graham crackers and press into the bottom of an 8-inch round springform pan, or a pan that fits into your slow cooker.

2. Puree or mash half the strawberries and beat together with the cheese, sugar, eggs, cornflour, lemon rind, and lemon juice until smooth.

3. Transfer the mixture into the pan and place in the slow cooker. Cover and cook on high for about 2 hours, or until almost set.

4. Turn off the slow cooker and let the cheesecake sit in the cooker for 2 hours. Remove and cool completely, then carefully turn out of the pan.

5. Decorate with the remaining sliced strawberries and serve.

CARROT CAKE

serves **8–10**

1 cup all-purpose flour
1 teaspoon baking soda
¼ teaspoon salt
½ teaspoon ground cinnamon
pinch of ground nutmeg
2 extra-large eggs
½ cup granulated sugar
¼ cup firmly packed light brown sugar
¼ cup vegetable oil, plus extra
  for greasing
⅔ cup buttermilk
1 teaspoon vanilla extract
4 cups shredded carrots
1 cup shredded dry coconut
¼ cup golden raisins (optional)
whipped cream, to serve

A 3¾-quart, round or oval slow cooker is perfect for this moist and delicious cake. If using a larger or smaller slow cooker, the cooking time may need to be adjusted. After 1½ hours of cooking, check every 15 minutes to see if the cake is ready.

1. Grease the inside of the slow cooker with oil.

2. Put the flour, baking soda, salt, cinnamon, and nutmeg into a small bowl and mix to combine. Put the eggs, granulated sugar, and brown sugar into medium bowl and beat together until well combined. Add the oil, buttermilk, and vanilla extract and stir to combine. Add the egg mixture to the flour mixture and mix well. Fold in the carrots and coconut, and the golden raisins, if using.

3. Pour the batter into the prepared slow cooker. Place several sheets of paper towels on top of the slow cooker, then put the lid on top to secure the paper towels in place above the cake batter. Cook on low for about 2 hours, until a toothpick inserted into the center of the cake comes out clean.

4. Keeping the cake in the ceramic insert, remove it from the slow cooker and transfer to a wire rack to cool for at least 30 minutes. Cut the cake into wedges and serve it directly from the insert. Serve warm or at room temperature with a dollop of whipped cream.

RICE PUDDING

serves **4**

¾ cup short-grain rice
4 cups milk
½ cup granulated sugar
1 teaspoon vanilla extract
ground cinnamon, for dusting

Creamy rice pudding flavored with vanilla is delicious served simply. Add a handful of dried fruit to the mixture for a change, or top with a little maple syrup before serving.

1. Rinse the rice well under cold running water and drain thoroughly. Pour the milk into a large, heavy saucepan, add the sugar, and bring to a boil, stirring continuously. Sprinkle in the rice, stir well, and simmer gently for 10–15 minutes. Transfer the mixture to a heatproof dish and cover with aluminum foil.

2. Stand the dish on a trivet in the slow cooker and pour in enough boiling water to come about one-third of the way up the side of the dish. Cover and cook on high for 2 hours.

3. Remove the dish from the slow cooker and discard the foil. Stir the vanilla extract into the rice, then spoon it into warm bowls. Lightly dust with cinnamon and serve immediately.

MINI PUMPKIN CHEESECAKES WITH GINGERSNAP CRUST

serves **4**

Crust
1 cup crushed gingersnaps
2 tablespoons packed light brown sugar
pinch of salt
3 tablespoons unsalted butter, melted

Filling
1 tablespoon flour
¼ teaspoon ground cinnamon
pinch of grated nutmeg
pinch of salt
2 extra-large eggs
½ cup firmly packed light brown sugar
½ cup cream cheese
1 cup canned pumpkin puree
2 tablespoons heavy cream
2 teaspoons vanilla extract
1 tablespoon whiskey
confectioners' sugar, for dusting

Spicy gingersnaps provide a crunchy crust for a rich, pumpkin-flavored cheesecake filling.

1. To make the crust, preheat the oven to 375°F. Put the crushed gingersnaps, sugar, and salt into a food processor and pulse several times. Add the butter and pulse until well combined. Press the mixture into the bottoms and about three-quarters of the way up the sides of four 1-cup ramekins. Put the ramekins onto a baking sheet and bake in the preheated oven for 10 minutes. Let cool.

2. To make the filling, put the flour, cinnamon, nutmeg, and salt into a large bowl and beat together. Beat in the eggs, sugar, cream cheese, pumpkin puree, cream, vanilla extract, and whiskey.

3. Spoon the filling into the ramekins and place the ramekins in the slow cooker. Carefully add boiling water to a depth of 1½ inches. Cover and cook on high for about 2 hours, until the filling is set. Turn off the slow cooker and let the ramekins stand inside for an additional 1 hour, then remove them from the slow cooker and chill in the refrigerator for at least 2 hours. Dust with confectioners' sugar before serving.

CHOCOLATE PUDDINGS

serves **6**

1¼ cups light cream
1¼ cups milk
8 ounces semisweet chocolate,
  broken into small pieces
1 extra-large egg
4 egg yolks
¼ cup granulated sugar
⅔ cup heavy cream
chocolate curls, to decorate

A favorite dessert for chocolate lovers. Make this recipe the day before to let the chocolate set firmly and become gooey.

1. Pour the light cream and milk into a saucepan and add the chocolate. Set the pan over low heat and stir until the chocolate has melted and the mixture is smooth. Remove from the heat and let cool for 10 minutes.

2. Beat together the egg, egg yolks, and sugar in a bowl until combined. Gradually stir in the chocolate mixture until thoroughly blended, then strain into a small bowl.

3. Divide the mixture among six ramekins and cover with aluminum foil. Stand the ramekins on a trivet in the slow cooker and pour in enough boiling water to come about halfway up the sides of the ramekins. Cover and cook on low for 3–3½ hours, until just set. Remove the slow cooker insert and let cool completely, then remove the ramekins and chill in the refrigerator for at least 4 hours.

4. Whip the heavy cream in a bowl until it holds soft peaks. Top each chocolate pudding with a little of the whipped cream and decorate with chocolate curls. Serve immediately.

STUFFED APPLES

serves **4**

4 large Granny Smith or other
  cooking apples
¾ cup firmly packed light brown sugar
¼ cup rolled oats
1 teaspoon ground cinnamon
4 tablespoons butter, cut into
  small pieces
2 tablespoons golden raisins
¼ cup coarsely chopped pecans
  or walnuts
whipped cream, to serve

This simple dessert is a lot healthier than apple pie, but just as delicious.

1. Use a paring knife to cut the stem end out of each apple, then scoop out the core with a melon baller or teaspoon, leaving the bottom of the apple intact.

2. To make the filling, put the sugar, oats, cinnamon, and butter into a bowl and mix together with a fork. Add the golden raisins and nuts and toss to mix well. Stuff the mixture into the apples, dividing it evenly.

3. Pour ½ cup of water into the slow cooker, then carefully add the apples, standing them up in the bottom of the slow cooker. Cover and cook on high for about 1½ hours or on low for 3 hours. Serve the apples hot, topped with whipped cream.

POACHED PEACHES IN WINE

serves **4–6**

⅔ cup Marsala wine
¾ cup water
¼ cup granulated sugar
1 vanilla bean, split lengthwise
6 peaches, cut into wedges and pitted
2 teaspoon cornstarch
crème fraîche or Greek yogurt, to serve

Marsala is a fortified wine from Sicily, similar to port. Use it in dessert recipes, such as tiramisu, or with fruit, such as peaches and nectarines.

1. Pour the Marsala wine and ⅔ cup of the water into a saucepan and add the sugar and vanilla bean. Set the pan over low heat and stir until the sugar has dissolved, then bring to a boil without stirring. Remove from the heat.

2. Put the peaches into the slow cooker and pour the syrup over them. Cover and cook on high for 1–1½ hours, until the fruit is tender.

3. Using a slotted spoon, gently transfer the peaches to a serving dish. Remove the vanilla bean from the slow cooker and scrape the seeds into the syrup with the point of a knife. Discard the bean. Stir the cornstarch to a paste with the remaining water in a small bowl, then stir into the syrup. Replace the lid and cook on high for 15 minutes, stirring occasionally.

4. Spoon the syrup over the fruit and let cool slightly. Serve warm or chill in the refrigerator for 2 hours before serving with crème fraîche or yogurt.

CARAMELIZED BANANA UPSIDE-DOWN CAKE

serves **6–8**

1½ cups all-purpose flour
¼ cup firmly packed light brown sugar
¾ cup granulated sugar
¾ teaspoon baking soda
½ teaspoon baking powder
½ teaspoon salt
3 tablespoons unsalted butter
2 ripe bananas
½ cup buttermilk
1 teaspoon vanilla extract
2 eggs

Caramelized banana
5 tablespoons unsalted butter
¾ cup firmly packed light brown sugar
pinch of salt
2 small ripe bananas, sliced

This retro-hip 1950s throwback is easy to make, fun to serve, and delicious to eat.

1. To make the caramelized banana, put the butter into a 7-inch soufflé dish and place it in the microwave on high for about 1 minute, until melted. Tilt the dish to coat the sides and bottom with the butter, then stir in the sugar and the salt. Spread the mixture evenly over the bottom of the dish. Add the sliced bananas on top, ideally in a single layer, or overlapping slightly if necessary.

2. Put the flour, brown sugar, granulated sugar, baking soda, baking powder, and salt into a medium bowl and mix to combine. Put the butter into a large bowl and place it in the microwave on high for about 1 minute, until melted. Add the bananas and mash them into the butter. Beat in the buttermilk, vanilla extract, and eggs. Add the flour mixture to the butter mixture and beat until thoroughly combined.

3. Pour the cake batter over the sliced bananas in the soufflé dish and place in the slow cooker on a trivet. Cover and cook on low for 2 hours, until cooked through. Turn off the cooker and let the cake stand in it for an additional 30 minutes.

4. Keeping the soufflé dish in the ceramic insert, remove them both from the slow cooker and transfer to a wire rack to cool for 15 minutes. Run a thin knife around the edge of the cake to release it from the sides of the dish, then turn it out onto a serving platter. Slice into wedges and serve.

ITALIAN BREAD PUDDING

serves **6**

unsalted butter, for greasing
6 slices panettone
3 tablespoons Marsala wine
1¼ cups milk
1¼ cups light cream
½ cup granulated sugar
grated rind of ½ lemon
pinch of ground cinnamon
3 extra-large eggs, lightly beaten

A great variation on traditional bread-and-butter pudding. Panettone is an Italian fruit loaf available mainly at Christmas time, but you can use any sweet fruit bread or brioche.

1. Grease a 1-quart, deep round ovenproof dish with butter. Place the panettone on a deep plate and sprinkle with the Marsala wine.

2. Pour the milk and cream into a saucepan and add the sugar, lemon rind, and cinnamon. Gradually bring to a boil over low heat, stirring until the sugar has dissolved. Remove the pan from the heat and let cool slightly, then pour the mixture onto the eggs, beating continuously.

3. Place the panettone in the prepared ovenproof dish, pour in the egg mixture, and cover with aluminum foil. Stand the dish on a trivet in the slow cooker and pour in enough boiling water to come about one-third of the way up the sides of the dish. Cover and cook on high for 2½ hours, until set.

4. Carefully remove the dish from the slow cooker and discard the foil. Let cool, then chill in the refrigerator until required. Run a knife around the inside of the dish, then turn out onto a serving dish. Serve immediately.

BUTTERSCOTCH PUDDINGS

serves **6**

2 tablespoons unsalted butter
1¼ cups firmly packed dark brown sugar
½ teaspoon salt
1¼ cups heavy cream
¾ cup milk
4 egg yolks, lightly beaten
2 teaspoons vanilla extract
2 teaspoons whiskey
whipped cream, to serve

These rich and creamy butterscotch puddings are a cinch to make in the slow cooker.

1. Fill the slow cooker with water to a depth of about 1½ inches.

2. Melt the butter in a large saucepan over medium heat. Add the sugar and salt and stir to mix well. Add the cream and milk and heat over medium heat, until hot but not boiling.

3. Put the egg yolks into a medium mixing bowl. Add the sugar-and-milk mixture in a thin stream, whisking continuously. Whisk in the vanilla extract and whiskey. Ladle the mixture into six ½-cup ramekins.

4. Carefully place the ramekins in the slow cooker, being careful not to slosh any of the water into them. Cover the slow cooker and cook on low for about 2 hours, or until the puddings are set.

5. Remove the ramekins from the slow cooker and transfer to a wire rack to cool for about 15 minutes, then cover with plastic wrap, put into the refrigerator, and chill for at least 2 hours before serving. Serve chilled, topped with a spoonful of whipped cream.

CHOCOLATE CAKE

serves **8**

13 ounces semisweet chocolate,
 broken into pieces
1½ sticks unsalted butter,
 plus extra for greasing
¾ cup firmly packed light brown sugar
4 eggs
2 teaspoons vanilla extract
1¼ cups all-purpose flour
1¼ teaspoons baking powder
½ cup ground almonds (almond meal)
½ cup heavy cream
confectioners' sugar, for dusting

Everyone loves chocolate cake, and this recipe will become a favorite. For a special occasion, sprinkle fresh raspberries on top of the filling.

1. Place a trivet or a ring of crumpled aluminum foil in the bottom of the slow cooker. Grease and line the bottom of a deep, 8-inch diameter cake pan, or a pan that fits into your slow cooker.

2. Melt 9 ounces of the chocolate in a bowl set over a saucepan of simmering water. Remove from the heat and cool slightly.

3. Beat the butter and sugar in a large bowl until pale and fluffy. Gradually beat in the eggs. Stir in the melted chocolate and 1 teaspoon of vanilla extract. Fold in the flour, baking powder, and almonds evenly.

4. Spoon the batter into the pan, spreading it evenly. Place in the slow cooker, cover, and cook on high for 2½ hours or until risen and springy to the touch.

5. Remove from the slow cooker and let the cake stand in the pan for 10 minutes. Turn out and cool on a wire rack.

6. Put the remaining chocolate and vanilla extract with the cream into a saucepan and heat gently, stirring, until melted. Cool until thick enough to spread. Split the cake into two layers and sandwich together with the filling. Dust with confectioners' sugar to serve.

APPLE CRISP

serves **4–6**

½ cup granulated sugar
1 tablespoon cornstarch
1 teaspoon ground cinnamon
¼ teaspoon ground nutmeg
6 large Granny Smith or other cooking
  apples, peeled, cored, and chopped
2 tablespoons lemon juice
vanilla ice cream, to serve (optional)

Topping
½ cup all-purpose flour
⅓ cup firmly packed light brown sugar
3 tablespoons granulated sugar
pinch of salt
3 tablespoons unsalted butter,
  cut into small pieces
⅔ cup rolled oats
¾ cup coarsely chopped pecans
  or walnuts

This simple dessert will fill your house with the sweet smell of fall, and it's the perfect way to end a meal on a chilly evening.

1. Put the sugar, cornstarch, cinnamon, and nutmeg into the slow cooker and stir to combine. Add the apples and lemon juice and toss to coat well.

2. To make the topping, put the flour, brown sugar, granulated sugar, and salt into a large mixing bowl and mix to combine. Using two knives, cut the butter into the flour mixture until it resembles coarse crumbs. Add the oats and nuts and toss until well combined.

3. Sprinkle the topping evenly over the apple mixture, cover, and cook on high for about 2 hours or on low for about 4 hours, until the apples are soft. Set the lid ajar and cook for an additional 1 hour, or until the topping is crisp. Serve warm, topped with vanilla ice cream, if using.

BLUSHING PEARS

serves **6**

6 small ripe pears
1 cup ruby port
1 cup granulated sugar
1 teaspoon finely chopped crystallized
  ginger
2 tablespoons lemon juice
whipped cream or Greek yogurt, to serve

A port-flavored syrup tints the pears a delicate pink color as they cook. You can use Madeira wine instead of port and replace the ginger with a cinnamon stick.

1. Peel the pears, cut them in half lengthwise, and scoop out the cores. Place them in the slow cooker.

2. Combine the port, sugar, ginger, and lemon juice in a small bowl and pour the mixture over the pears. Cover and cook on low for 4 hours, until the pears are tender.

3. Let the pears cool in the slow cooker, then carefully transfer to a bowl and chill in the refrigerator until required.

4. To serve, cut each pear half into about six slices lengthwise, leaving the fruit intact at the stem end. Carefully lift the pear halves onto serving plates and press gently to fan out the slices. Spoon the cooking juices over the pears and serve immediately with cream.

GINGER CAKE

serves **8–10**

1 stick unsalted butter, melted,
   plus extra for greasing
¹/₃ cup firmly packed light brown sugar
¹/₃ cup light corn syrup
1 teaspoon vanilla extract
1¹/₃ cups all-purpose flour
2 teaspoons ground ginger
1¹/₂ teaspoons baking soda
pinch of salt
2 extra-large eggs, lightly beaten
¹/₂ cup milk
whipped cream, to serve

This moist, spicy ginger cake is even better the day after it is made. After cooling, cover loosely with aluminum foil and store at room temperature.

1. Grease the bottom and sides of a7-inch soufflé dish. Fill the slow cooker with hot (not boiling) water to a depth of about 1 inch.

2. Put the butter, sugar, corn syrup, and vanilla extract into a medium bowl and stir to mix well. Put the flour, ginger, baking soda, and salt into a large mixing bowl and stir to combine. Stir the butter mixture into the flour mixture with a wooden spoon and mix together until well combined. Add the eggs and milk and continue to mix until smooth.

3. Pour the batter into the prepared soufflé dish and carefully place it in the slow cooker. Cover and cook on low for about 3 hours, until a toothpick inserted into the center of the cake comes out clean. Keeping the soufflé dish in the ceramic insert, remove them both from the slow cooker and transfer to a wire rack to cool for at least 30 minutes, then remove the soufflé dish from the insert and let cool for an additional 30 minutes.

4. To serve, slice the cake into wedges and top with a spoonful of whipped cream.

ALMOND CHARLOTTE

serves **4**

unsalted butter, for greasing
10–12 ladyfingers
1¼ cups milk
2 eggs
2 tablespoons granulated sugar
⅓ cup blanched almonds, chopped
4–5 drops of almond extract

Sherry sauce
1 tablespoon granulated sugar
3 egg yolks
⅔ cup cream sherry

1. Grease a round, 2½-cup ovenproof dish with butter. Line the dish with the ladyfingers, cutting them to fit and placing them cut-ends down and sugar-coated sides outward. Cover the bottom of the dish with some of the scraps.

2. Pour the milk into a saucepan and bring just to a boil, then remove from the heat. Beat together the eggs and sugar in a heatproof bowl until combined, then stir in the milk. Stir in the almonds and almond extract.

3. Carefully pour the batter into the prepared dish, making sure that the ladyfingers stay in place, and cover with aluminum foil. Stand the dish on a trivet in the slow cooker and pour in enough boiling water to come about halfway up the sides of the dish. Cover and cook on high for 3–3½ hours, until set.

4. Shortly before serving, make the sherry sauce. Put the sugar, egg yolks, and sherry into a heatproof bowl. Set the bowl over a saucepan of simmering water, without letting the bottom of the bowl touch the surface of the water. Whisk well until the mixture thickens, but do not let it boil. Remove from the heat.

5. Carefully remove the dish from the slow cooker and discard the foil. Let stand for 2–3 minutes, then turn out onto a warm serving plate. Pour the sherry sauce around it and serve immediately.

CHOCOLATE FONDUE

serves **4–6**

butter, for greasing
1 cup heavy cream
12 ounces semisweet chocolate,
  chopped into small pieces
1 teaspoon vanilla extract

To serve
diced fruit (bananas, strawberries,
  apples, pears)
marshmallows
cookies or pieces of cake

This easy-to-make, yet decadent dessert is a fun way to end a dinner party.

1. Grease the inside of the slow cooker with butter.

2. Put the cream and chocolate into the slow cooker and stir to combine. Cover and cook on low, stirring occasionally, for 45–60 minutes, until the chocolate is completely melted. Stir in the vanilla extract.

3. Keep the mixture in the slow cooker or transfer it to a fondue pot with a burner and serve immediately, with platters of diced fruit, marshmallows, and cookies for dipping.